BUILDING A
MINI
2001 onwards (all models)

First published in September 2017

A catalogue record for this book is available
from the British Library.

ISBN 978 1 78521 112 6

Library of Congress control no. 2016959370

Published by Haynes Publishing,
Sparkford, Yeovil,
Somerset BA22 7JJ, UK.
Tel: 01963 440635
Int. tel: +44 1963 440635
Website: www.haynes.com

Haynes North America Inc.,
859 Lawrence Drive, Newbury Park,
California 91320, USA.

Printed in Malaysia.

BUILDING A
MINI

2001 onwards (all models)

Operations Manual

An insight into the manufacture and production
of the MINI at Plant Oxford

Chris Randall

Contents

Foreword

People often talk about a car's DNA and I am in no doubt that the genes of the classic Mini, produced here in Cowley from 1959 to 1968, are present in the MINIs we build today.

A small car that makes the maximum use of space, that trademark 'go-kart' feel, and the presence of various design icons, inside and outside the car, that give a respectful nod to its heritage. What you have today is not just a very special-looking car with a unique, up-to-date design, but one in which you still feel, touch, see and experience the central ideas that were behind the original. To successfully oversee that kind of evolution, without forgetting the pedigree of the past, is not an easy thing to do; in fact I would say that it is quite rare – in the motoring world at least.

Everyone who loves this car has their own story about how their fascination with it started. Mine began when I was maybe seven or eight years old, when I was growing up in Zurich. There was a young woman who lived next door and she had a beautiful red classic Mini. I remember looking down the street in anticipation of seeing it whizzing down the road and pulling into the driveway.

From that point on I became fascinated with this little car and a few years later I found my way into engineering. After spending more than half of my career in an assembly-focused environment, I now oversee production at our plants in Swindon and in Oxford – the place we call the 'heart and home' of MINI.

This plant, one of the oldest mass production car plants in the world, has an almost mythical status in the UK and beyond – and working here gives you a real sense of privilege. By the time you read this, Plant Oxford will have built well over three million MINIs. That is a phenomenal achievement and one that everyone associated with this place can be proud of.

We have a deeply committed workforce, with a passion for the plant and for the brand. There is also a shared sense of history, one that is keenly felt by the multi-generational families working here. BMW has, of course, invested heavily to deliver a truly state-of-the-art facility. But without a dedicated and driven team of people, we couldn't have achieved all that we have in recent years.

No one single production process is any more important than another. It is essential to get *all* of them right in order to produce the highest quality cars. But if you ask me what my favourite part of it all is, well, I'd have to say that it's seeing a finished car rolling off the line. That is a special sight – no matter how often you see it.

I know that Chris Randall has worked closely with our team to produce what is a fascinating and, perhaps, the most in-depth look ever into life here at Plant Oxford and how MINIs are built.

I hope you enjoy reading this book at least half as much as we enjoy building the cars.

Frank Bachmann, Managing Director
April 2017

Acknowledgements

To be honest, it's very hard to know where to start, as so many people have been incredibly generous with their time and help, not to mention very patient as I attempted to get to grips with everything that goes on at Plant Oxford. It makes sense to begin there, then, and huge thanks must go to the communications team who showed immense support for this manual from the very beginning, and were instrumental in driving the project forward. Particular thanks go to Steve Wrelton, without whose tireless work and enthusiasm this manual couldn't have been written; his help was above and beyond the call of duty. And I must also thank Sarah Heaney and all of the people in her team for contributions and assistance. Not forgetting, of course, the Managing Director, Frank Bachmann, who kindly granted us such amazing access to the plant.

Then there are the many people at the sharp end of the fascinating work within Plant Oxford, Plant Swindon and Hams Hall, who generously shared their knowledge with me, including Roslyn Fordyce, Alex McKenzie; Andrew Robinson; Adam Broomhall; Gareth Davies; Greg Denton; Jim Eustace; Kate Bird; Roger Newman; Steve Prosser; Chris Brownridge; Tom Bennett; Kimberley Ragousis; Nicole Prinz; James Loukes; Dave Moriarty; Charles Selwood; Martin Sebon; Tim Coleman; Wayne Berry; Jeremy Stoyle; Paul Ricketts; Roberto Bonassisa; Tom Festa; Jagoda Stasiak; Nick Dear; and Yaminah Pupek. I realise that this isn't everyone that I've spoken to during the course of writing this manual, so to those whose names don't appear here I apologise and offer sincere thanks for your time and input. I should also add that their input included a huge number of facts that I've attempted to reproduce as accurately as possible – any mistakes are mine alone.

I must also thank the thousands of dedicated people at Plant Oxford who produce the car that I've had the pleasure of writing about within these pages; I'm sure I got in your way during my numerous visits, so apologies. And of course, I wouldn't have had the opportunity to write this book at all if it wasn't for Steve Rendle at Haynes Publishing. Not only did Steve provide endless support, enthusiasm and guidance along the way, but I also very much appreciate the faith he showed in me when we first began discussing this project.

Last but not least, huge thanks as always to my wife Rebecca, who has heard more about the intricacies of MINI production than any wife should really have to endure, and who showed great patience as I regaled her with yet more fascinating facts. I couldn't have done it without her unwavering support and encouragement.

Chris Randall
June 2017

Introduction

Haynes have spent more than 50 years producing detailed manuals that show owners how to take their cars apart and repair them – and I've been immensely privileged to have played my own small part in that – but this book was an opportunity to do something a little different. Why? Because this time the manual would be all about putting a car together, rather than taking one apart.

Building a modern car is a fascinating and complex business, one that takes thousands of people and a huge amount of knowledge and dedication to attain the sort of high quality, reliable and enjoyable cars that people want to buy. I for one wanted to find out how it's done,

and then be able to share a detailed insight with readers so that they, too, could understand just what happens inside one of the most modern and productive car factories in the world. Once inside, I'd be granted access to every aspect of the production process, not to mention the talented and committed people that make it all happen. That factory would be Plant Oxford, a place that's been at the heart of the British motor industry for more than a hundred years and has been responsible for some of the most evocative names ever to grace the automobile. Located just a few miles from the city, famous for its university, it is home to a brand loved by enthusiasts across the globe. That brand is MINI.

But why choose the MINI as the basis for this book? Well, you only have to look at the sheer number on our roads to realise just how popular the car is, so much so that just three years after production began the half-millionth example had already rolled out of the factory gates. And more have been doing so ever since, and at an ever-increasing rate, as buyers across the world clamour to get their hands on this stylish car; indeed, one of the many facts I learned during the writing of this book was that around 1,000 examples are built at the factory every day, which gives some idea of just how sought-after a MINI is.

That popularity wasn't always so certain, though, and when BMW decided to purchase the ailing Rover Group back in 1994 industry observers were perhaps more than a little apprehensive about how the successful German company would look after one of Britain's best-loved – if troubled – names. For the car you'll

↓ MINI production began at Plant Oxford in 2001. This is the first car to roll off the Plant Oxford production line, and the pride of everyone involved is obvious.

read about within these pages the answer would come in 2001 when, after selling Rover to a private consortium, BMW launched the MINI to an expectant public. Any doubts people may have had were washed away in a wave of enthusiasm for the new car, one that brought the much-loved original bang up to date; this was Sir Alec Issigonis' legendary car reinvented for the 21st century. If anyone needed a demonstration that BMW truly understood the brand, not to mention its significance to the British motor industry, this was it.

But it's not just the technical aspects of the project that fascinated me, although those are incredibly compelling. It's that understanding and careful nurturing of both the brand and, perhaps more importantly, the people that make it all happen that I wanted to discover and explain. I was first approached by Haynes about writing the book in the autumn of 2015 and was instantly thrilled by the idea, and I certainly wasn't going to need asking twice. As someone who's loved cars for more than 40 years and had their fair share of driving and attempting to repair (not always with great success, if I'm honest) classic Minis, the opportunity to immerse myself in the business of building the modern version wasn't one that I had any plans to pass up. But exciting as the idea was there still remained the task of persuading the powers that be at BMW that this was a story that was crying out to be told. Neither Haynes nor I should have worried, though, as it was clear from the very first mention that the company were as intrigued by the idea as we were.

Over the following weeks and months it quickly became apparent that the company were incredibly supportive of our plans to find out everything there was to know about building a modern MINI, and then some. This wasn't, I explained to them, intended to be a cursory look behind the scenes, oh no. Instead, this was a request for access to all aspects of Plant Oxford and the production processes that take place within it, not to mention as many of the key people as we could fit within these pages. And despite being inundated with requests to visit the factory by everyone from motoring magazines to television companies, let alone trying to concentrate on the rather complex task of actually building cars, still they said

yes. Since that very first contact everyone at BMW and the factory have demonstrated their commitment to helping us deliver the project, and for that I'm extremely grateful.

I've been fortunate enough to visit a number of car factories over the years, and it's an experience that has never failed to leave a lasting impression, not to mention a huge admiration for the talented people that keep us car enthusiasts supplied with the machines we love so much. If you thought it was just a case of bolting a few parts together and seeing a finished car roll out of the doors, then you might be surprised at what really happens within the walls of these busy, technologically advanced and exciting places. We've never before been inside a modern car factory to produce a Haynes manual, so it was a project that presented plenty of challenges, but we hope that this book proves as enjoyable to read as it was to write. You might not think of a modern car in quite the same way again...

↑ **Just some of the 1,000 cars produced every day that await transport to their excited new owners.**

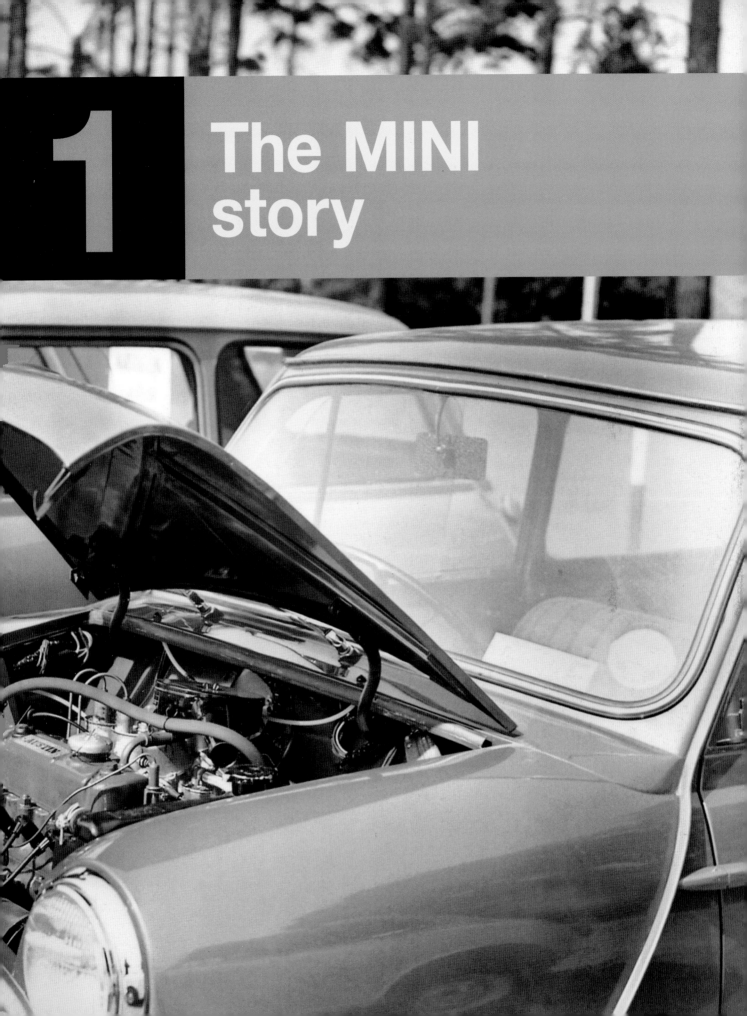

1 The MINI story

While this manual will soon delve into the detail of just what goes into building a modern MINI, it's worth taking a little time to consider the background to one of the most famous cars of all time. The story of the Mini's development is a fascinating one in itself, and a book like this wouldn't be complete without first taking a closer look at the people who were instrumental in its creation. And then, of course, there are the modern MINIs that have made this manual possible. Here, then, is the beginning of what these amazing cars are all about.

Alec Issigonis

Born in Turkey as Alexander Arnold Constantine Issigonis, the man better known simply as Alec is famous as being the father of the Mini. He arrived in London in 1922 with his mother Hulda Prokopp (who, rather neatly for this story, was related to Bernd Pischetsrieder, the BMW boss responsible for buying the Rover Group) and studied engineering at Battersea Polytechnic. By 1936, now a talented engineer, he had joined Morris Motors as a designer. Prior to his work on the Mini he was responsible for the Morris Minor, the first British car to achieve one million sales, but he also spent time at Alvis, working on both car and engine design.

The crucial moment in his career came in 1955, when he was approached by Leonard Lord of the British Motor Corporation (BMC), who wanted him to design a new range of models for the company. This was interrupted by the Suez crisis and the subsequent concerns over fuel shortages, which in turn led to BMC focusing on the introduction of smaller, more economical cars – and Issigonis had the perfect answer in the form of the Mini.

A clever man, he was known to be stubborn and not keen on taking advice, but there was one thing that he particularly disliked and that was things that were unnecessarily large. The perfect approach, he decided, was for a car to be no more than ten feet long yet be capable of seating four, with 80% of the car used for passenger space. It took some clever engineering to achieve those aims – notably the front-wheel-drive layout and a transverse engine with the gearbox located in the sump – but car enthusiasts have been enjoying the results ever since.

Promoted to Technical Director at BMC, Issigonis would also oversee the launch of the larger Austin 1100 and 1800 models, but company disagreements saw him become sidelined in later years, and after being knighted in 1969 he would leave what was then British Leyland in 1971.

Leonard Lord

Lord would play a key role in the Morris story at Cowley, having worked for Hotchkiss during World War One, which later became Morris Engines. By 1933 he was the Director of Morris Motors and was heavily involved in the modernisation of the Cowley plant and the use of mass production techniques for the cars made there. After falling out with William Morris (later Lord Nuffield) Lord resigned, and by 1938 had joined the Austin Motor Company, where he played a similar role in the development of the Longbridge factory. Following the merger of Austin and Morris into the British Motor Corporation in 1952, Lord became Chairman two years later and would soon make that important approach to Alec Issigonis.

Herbert Austin

Austin's engineering career would begin in Australia, to which he'd emigrated in 1882, aged 16. Working for the Wolseley Sheep Shearing Company, he returned to Birmingham to set up a tool manufacturing plant for the company but soon became interested in automobiles. Despite becoming manager of the Wolseley Tool and Motor Company Limited and overseeing the production of some early cars, he was keen to pursue his own ideas and became unhappy with the direction Wolseley were taking and the lack of finance. His answer was to set up the Austin Motor Company in 1905 with a factory at Longbridge, a place that would go on to produce some of the country's best-selling cars. It was long after his death in 1941 that his name would adorn the wonderful Mini.

History of the Mini through to BMW ownership

Concerns over fuel shortages in the wake of the Suez crisis had led a number of manufacturers to explore more fuel-efficient vehicles, and one of the results was the 'Bubble Car'. Cheap to buy and run these may have been, but BMC Chairman Leonard Lord hated them and wanted the company to build a proper alternative. First designated XC9003, the new small car would come to be known internally as ADO15 – the Mini. Work got under way in March 1957 with Alec Issigonis leading the development team, a small group that included Jack Daniels, who'd worked with him on the Morris Minor, Chris Kingham, a colleague from Alvis, and just a handful of other people.

The car's compact dimensions had been decided early in the project, with Issigonis stipulating that as well as the car being a maximum of ten feet long its engine had to take up no more than two feet of that, which meant a transverse installation; and the engine had to be one used in current production, which led to the adoption of the A-Series unit in 848cc form, a capacity reckoned to provide ample performance for the new model. Needless to say, such compact packaging would present plenty of challenges, amongst them the need to adopt tiny 10in wheels pushed out to each corner, which saw Dunlop develop special tyres.

Early testing discovered that the bodyshell

was prone to cracking under hard use, so subframes were used front and rear to carry the mechanical components and help spread the loads more evenly. And although the nose-heavy layout was good for stability it did reveal issues with the rear brakes locking, the answer to which was the use of a limiting valve to reduce hydraulic pressure at the rear along with moving the battery to the boot to help even up weight distribution. The compact rubber cone suspension system, developed by Alex Moulton, was also adopted for the Mini, and together with the transverse engine and gearbox-in-sump layout ensured that the new car hit its size targets perfectly.

The big question, though, was did it work? July 1957 saw Leonard Lord try a prototype and he very much liked what he found, telling Issigonis in no uncertain terms to get on with building it. Despite varying accounts of the story, it's widely accepted that production of the Austin Seven got under way at Longbridge in the first few days of May 1959 and the Morris Mini Minor at Cowley very shortly after that. It's worth noting that a car bearing the registration number 621 AOK was reckoned to be the very first example – Alec Issigonis being pictured with the car in reports of the time – but, although generally accepted, the reality is that almost half a dozen had been made prior to that.

The car was unveiled to the press on 18 and 19 August 1959 at the Chobham test track in Surrey – the launch budget was reportedly just £500 – and, while the car was well received,

PREVIOUS PAGES
The father of the Mini, Alec Issigonis, with one of his legendary creations. Launched in 1959, more than five million examples would be built.

⬇ An early prototype of the model initially known as XC9003. It's not quite the finished article, but those famous proportions are clear to see.

little did the assembled journalists realise that this was the beginning of a story that would continue for 41 years. Problems soon arose, however, not least around the issue of pricing. Profits on the new car would be non-existent for some years, not least because confusion between Austin and Morris saw the price being set incredibly low at just £496 – a figure that undercut rivals by a substantial margin. The price certainly amazed the likes of Ford, who famously bought a Mini, stripped it down and costed every component, discovering in the process that BMC was losing five pounds on every one it made. Still, sales were healthy thanks to the Mini's classless appeal, which attracted everyone, from cash-strapped family buyers to celebrities.

Production reached the half a million mark in December 1962, one million just three years later and an impressive three million by October 1972. Much of this was down to the wide range of models that were being launched, beginning with the van and pickup variants that arrived in 1960 and 1961 respectively. The latter year would also see the arrival of the booted and decidedly upmarket Riley Elf and Wolseley Hornet, and the Austin Seven Countryman and Morris Mini Traveller estates, not to mention the now legendary Cooper.

First suggested by race car maker John Cooper, the Mini Cooper would become famous both for its appearance on the big screen in *The Italian Job* and for its exploits on the Monte Carlo rally. It would win this tough event in 1964, 1965 and 1967, cruelly robbed of a third straight victory in 1966 after being disqualified over a rather dubious issue concerning its lights. The Cooper was a great success and would become the 1071S in 1963, with the 970S and 1275S arriving the following year along with the quirky utility model, the Moke.

October 1967 saw the introduction of the Mark 2 Mini that benefitted from a number of improvements including the adoption of hydrolastic (or 'wet') suspension for most models. In January 1968 production ended at Cowley, all Minis thereafter being built at Longbridge. One of the biggest changes of the time came in 1969, with not only the Mark 3 Mini (by now losing the external door hinges) but also the introduction of the 1275GT – to replace the Cooper – and the Clubman. Both cars featured a flat front end derived from the Austin Maxi that didn't meet with universal approval, although it didn't prevent production hitting the four million mark in 1976.

A decade later British Leyland became the Rover Group and Alec Issigonis passed away two years later, sadly not witnessing the huge changes that were soon to take place and bring us to where we are today. 1990 saw the relaunch of the Cooper name, signalling something of a renaissance for the Mini brand, and four years later the Rover Group were

→ This is a 1964 Super de Luxe model. Note the sliding front windows and external door hinges, both features that would disappear from later variants.

bought by BMW, who introduced what would be the final version of the much-loved car in 1996, a model that featured a fuel-injected 63bhp engine and even an airbag. But by October 2000 it was all over for the iconic little car, production ending after an amazing 5,378,776 had rolled out of the factory gates in Birmingham and Oxford. Luckily for us, however, a whole new chapter was just about to begin…

⬆ **Early production was very much a hands-on affair with little in the way of automation. It's a far cry from today's high-tech construction methods.**

⬅ The famous Mini Cooper S. A Mark II model from 1968, note the fillers on each rear wing for the twin fuel tanks.

MODELS PRODUCED SINCE 2001

MINI Hatch

Launched at the 2000 Paris Motor Show, the eagerly awaited new MINI went on sale in July 2001. With funky styling inside and out, and sharp handling thanks to its complex multi-link rear suspension, the Cooper used a 115bhp 1.6-litre 'Tritec' engine developed with Chrysler. With an Eaton supercharger, the Cooper S produced 163bhp, while the range would expand to include an entry-level 'One' variant with 90bhp. A diesel model arrived in July 2003 powered by a 75bhp Toyota engine. There was huge scope for personalisation, from a wide range of individual options to the popular 'Salt', 'Pepper' and 'Chili' packs.

MINI Convertible

A huge hit with buyers, the first model was launched at the 2004 Geneva Motor Show. Engines were shared with the Cooper/S, and there was an electrically operated fabric roof that could be partially or fully opened, while the external boot hinges were a nod to the original Mini. BMW engines replaced the Chrysler units in 2006, and the second-generation model arrived in 2009. The first diesel variant arrived in mid-2010, and in 2016 the third generation car was launched; bigger and more spacious, its choice of engines included efficient three-cylinder units.

MINI Hatch

Outwardly similar to the original MINI, the 2006 second generation model was very different under the skin. With larger dimensions (it was 60mm longer), the front structure was all-new, the boot was larger and the interior boasted a more premium feel. The Chrysler engines were replaced with 'Prince' units co-developed by BMW and PSA Peugeot/Citroën, and although the Cooper S was now turbocharged rather than supercharged it retained the bonnet air scoop that identified the model. The R56 model was updated in 2010 with tweaks to the exterior styling and a revised interior featuring a wider range of equipment.

MINI Clubman

Drawing on a name from the past, MINI launched its estate model in June 2007. Available with petrol and diesel engines, it offered 930 litres of luggage space with the rear seats folded and featured split 'barn-style' doors for the load area. However, most notable was the 'Club door', a single small door on the right-hand side for rear passenger access; not ideally placed for right-hand-drive models, its positioning was due to the prohibitive cost of relocating the fuel filler on the opposite side. A brand new Clubman arrived in 2015, the biggest MINI yet, which featured conventional rear passenger doors and 'TwinPower' turbocharged engines. Available with ALL4 four-wheel drive, the new model also boasted another MINI first – an eight-speed automatic transmission.

MINI JCW

Inspired by the MINI Challenge race car and launched in July 2008, the John Cooper Works offered plenty of performance thanks to its turbocharged 211bhp engine. Unique styling features, aerodynamic improvements and uprated brakes and suspension all featured, and it was also available in Clubman and Convertible body styles. A limited edition 'GP' model in 2012 boasted 215bhp, just two seats and a 150mph top speed. A new model was unveiled at the 2015 Detroit Motor Show featuring a 228bhp 2.0-litre turbocharged engine and a host of performance and handling upgrades. The JCW badge now runs across the model range.

MINI Countryman

The five-door, five-seat model was available with petrol or diesel engines and a choice of two-wheel drive or ALL4 four-wheel drive, while a sportier JCW version arrived in 2012 featuring styling upgrades and more performance. Late 2016 saw the launch of the second generation model, featuring larger dimensions and also the first MINI to offer a plug-in hybrid drivetrain.

MINI Coupe

Revealed as a design concept in 2009, the production Coupe was launched at the 2011 Frankfurt Motor Show. A strict two-seater, it used the structure from the Convertible but featured a lightweight aluminium roof and a large tailgate for access to the luggage area. With retuned suspension, it was available with petrol and diesel engines including the 208bhp unit in the JCW variant. In February 2015 the company announced that production of both the Coupe and Roadster would be ending.

MINI Roadster

Based on the Coupe, and still with just two seats, the Roadster was unveiled at the 2012 Detroit Motor Show. Like the hardtop model, it featured an electrically extending rear spoiler, and there was an electrically operated fabric roof (standard for UK models) that folded away in 18 seconds at speeds of up to 20mph. It ended production in 2015 along with the Coupe.

MINI Paceman

Essentially a two-door Countryman with a more coupe-like roofline, the Paceman was launched at the 2012 Paris Motor Show. Offered with the same range of petrol and diesel engines, it could be had in two- or four-wheel-drive forms. Buyers could also opt for the rapid JCW model. However, neither buyers nor the motoring press were entirely convinced by the styling and the Paceman's position within the range, and sales were modest. MINI announced that production would cease at the end of 2016.

MINI Hatch (from 2014)

The third generation MINI was based on BMW's UKL1 platform and was longer, wider and taller than the outgoing model. Engines for the Cooper and diesel versions were all-new 1.5-litre three-cylinder units with 134bhp and 94bhp respectively, while the Cooper S used a 2.0-litre 189bhp motor. Highlights included an optional electronic damping system, a larger 211-litre boot and a well-equipped interior that retained all of the MINI style that buyers loved.

MINI Five-Door (from 2014)

Another first for the MINI brand, the five-door model was longer and taller and boasted a longer wheelbase than the three-door hatchback. Going on sale in autumn 2014, its extra space and practicality allowed the MINI to challenge established family rivals from mainstream car makers. Powered by 'TwinPower' turbocharged petrol and diesel engines, the new model featured plenty of driver assistance and connectivity options.

2 Designing a MINI

Redesigning a car as iconic as the original Mini was never going to be an easy task. Car design and technology had changed beyond all recognition in the decades since the launch of the original and, with stringent new regulations looming, it was a problem that Rover were already beginning to tackle by the 1990s. BMW's purchase of Rover in 1994 was an additional challenge, so it was fortunate that then BMW CEO Bernd Pischetsrieder – a great-nephew of Alec Issigonis – was fully behind the project that was officially known as the R50.

Design work was taking place in both the UK and Munich, the latter under the leadership of Chris Bangle, whose controversial 'flame surfacing' design themes would significantly influence the look of future BMWs. But a decision was needed, one that was taken in October 1995 at the Heritage Motor Centre at Gaydon, Warwickshire, when a number of models from both Rover and BMW were presented for judgement by senior company figures. One of the initial proposals had been produced by American designer Frank Stephenson, and this was the one chosen for development.

Renamed as the R50 project in May 1996, the continued involvement of both Rover and BMW was presenting major challenges and was a situation that needed to be addressed if the project was to have any chance of progressing. Indeed, attempts to resolve the internal politics would see all development pass to BMW in 1999. Their sale of MG-Rover the following year would present a further interruption, but BMW retained the project for the new car that would now become the MINI.

Plans were quickly made to arrange for production to take place at Oxford rather than at Longbridge, a decision that wasn't entirely well received by some people involved in the project. That controversy aside, the new model was well received by the public and motoring press alike after an official launch at the 2000 Paris Motor Show, and went on sale in the UK in July 2001. The rest, as they say, is history. And, of course, it was the beginning of a new era that would bring us to today and the content of this manual.

The design brief

We've mentioned Alec Issigonis' dislike of large cars elsewhere in this book, and his aim to make the original Mini as compact and space-efficient as possible. But things have changed a lot in the automotive world in the intervening 50 years, so just how do you set about designing a car such as this for the modern age – one that reflects the tastes of today's buyers when it comes to space, refinement and comfort, not to mention the demands of safety legislation? And, far more importantly, make it a MINI that delivers the style that fans of the brand will expect?

Well, for one thing the new car needs to be both instantly recognisable and reflect the way a MINI feels and drives, but at the same time be distinguishable from other models within the range. So the design process begins with plenty of research, sketching and brainstorming as the designers seek to understand the very character and essence of what makes each new model of MINI special. Clearly, heritage plays a big part in this and provides a strong guideline as to how a new model might look; it also helps to provide an emotional link with the original Mini. But the designers will take inspiration from a wide range

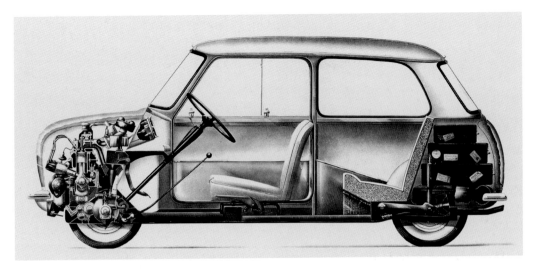

of sources, such as the worlds of fashion and architecture. However, as the designers make clear, their job is very much about developing a spiritual successor to those early models, one that transfers that innate character to a modern car, so it's important that they don't feel constrained by the past.

While the formal commission for a new model will already have been agreed, led by the new model's position within the MINI range or within the wider automotive sector (for example, the development of a new hatchback or an SUV), there are a number of tools that designers will use to help inform their work before any actual designing takes place. This can be in the form of market research with current and future customers (often referred to as 'customer clinics'), or the feedback received from the showing of design studies. Many of us will have seen design concepts at motor shows or in motoring magazines, and while many of them can appear very futuristic they are a useful way for designers to explore a new look or theme, elements of which can then be included in forthcoming models if they are well received by the public.

The design teams

The responsibility for designing a new MINI model falls to a surprisingly small number of people. At the time of writing this manual the MINI design team consists of around 30 designers working across three key disciplines and teams: the exterior; the interior; and colour and trim design. Heading those teams are Christopher Weil (head of exterior design MINI),

Oliver Sieghart (head of interior design MINI) and, as of September 2016, Kerstin Schmeding (head of colour and trim design MINI). Each team has around eight to ten members – so, for example, the ten colour and trim designers specialise in certain areas such as leather, car paint, graining and surfaces, and work in small project groups. Exterior and interior designers usually sketch the whole car and also oversee the integration of design and engineering until the car goes into production.

The challenges

It's probably fair to say that the history surrounding the brand means that MINI designers face more challenges than most when it comes to developing a new model. For

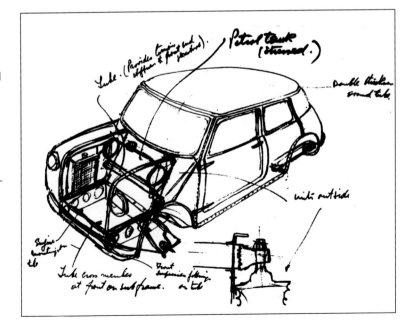

↑ Many hours are spent discussing and fine-tuning the colours, textures, and materials that will appear in the finished car.

one thing they need to maintain a firm link with the original principles – the transverse engine, the wheel at each corner stance, the go-kart feel on the road and the compact proportions, despite the obvious increase in size. Then they must ensure that the car both fulfils the specific design brief in terms of functionality and ergonomics and reflects the brand's future design direction.

In addition there are complex legislative requirements that govern everything, from environmental efficiency to passenger and pedestrian safety. Ever-stricter pedestrian safety rules have influenced the look of modern cars, especially at the front where the need for taller bodywork and space between bodywork and mechanical parts have to be factored in. However, rather than being seen as problems it's interesting that many designers view these challenges as a positive influence on their work, encouraging greater creativity when it comes to incorporating new technologies and regulations.

As well as technical challenges there are also aesthetic ones. The designers face a tough task in ensuring that each new model not only successfully interprets the classic Mini look for the modern age, but that it also retains the essential element of 'Britishness' that made the original so successful. And that's not all, as issues such as future technology and sustainability all have to be considered.

The design team are always keen to experiment with new technologies and surfaces, and are currently exploring what they term 'Industry 4.0' techniques such as 3D printing. But take the interior of a new model, for example – while there's a keen desire to experiment with and incorporate new materials, textures and finishes, many months of testing are required before they can be considered for a production car. In the case of seat materials those tests will focus on issues such as resistance to abrasion, tensile strength, colour fastness and resistance to fading under light. However, the designers also look to combine the use of classic materials, like leather, with new surfaces to capture the right MINI spirit; classic with a modern twist.

It's little easier when it comes to the exterior, the designers having to consider not just current customer preferences in areas such as paint colour but also to look ahead to how future trends might evolve. It can take up to three years to introduce a new colour once the testing of pigments and materials is taken into account, so an ability to look into the future is a key part of the designer's role. Ultimately all of these factors make for a delicate balancing act and it's clear that a lot of responsibility rests on designers if the final model is to be both successful and profitable.

Sketches

Go back to the earlier days of the Cowley plant's existence – and most other car makers come to that – and you'd likely have found vast rooms of draughtsmen hunched over drawing boards as they produced detailed renderings of every aspect of a new model. It was a very labour-intensive business, and while the advent of technology has changed things immeasurably hand-drawn sketches are still very much a part of the process when it comes to a new car. That's certainly true at MINI, where every design begins with hand-drawn sketches on a computer. A huge number of sketches will be made for both the exterior and interior, the first of which help designers to establish what they refer to as the 'bandwidth' or 'conceptual framework' for the styling – the essential parameters that will guide the finished design.

The earliest sketches will often be nothing

→ **Hand-drawn sketches are still a crucial first step in the design of a new MINI, allowing designers to explore the overall proportions as well as eye-catching details.**

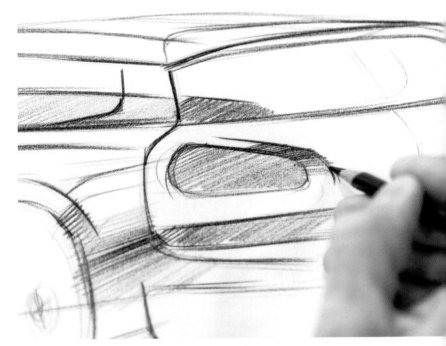

more than broad outlines, with detail added as the design develops. Focusing on settling the fundamental proportions that will make a new MINI instantly recognisable – externally for example, the relationship between the body, the glasshouse and the contrast roof – as well as pushing the boundaries when it comes to looks – up to ten designers from the MINI studio in Munich, as well as from the BMW Designworks studio in the United States, can be involved in the internal competition that takes place. However, this number will reduce as the sketched designs are regularly reviewed by the Head of Design, although everyone involved is keen that their design should be the one chosen!

With the exterior sketches whittled down to a smaller number of potential designs, a detailed review process is undertaken by senior figures, after which up to four designs progress to the next stage, which is 'tape drawings'. These have long been used when it comes to designing cars and still work effectively today. What happens is that a skilled team will transfer the sketches into full-sized outlines formed in flexible, black adhesive tape and presented on a white wall. This process allows designers to analyse the key dimensions and proportions in much greater detail. Using tape in this way allows the team to make alterations to an outline and instantly see how changes will influence the overall look.

Modelling

Once again, this stage of the process applies to the design of both the exterior and interior of a new model, with work being undertaken in parallel. It's also one of the most important

↗ **Interior design is as important as the exterior; this final design is the product of many hours of prior sketch work.**

→ **Tape drawings might seem old-fashioned, but they form an important part of the design process. They make it easier to view changes to shapes and forms before work progresses.**

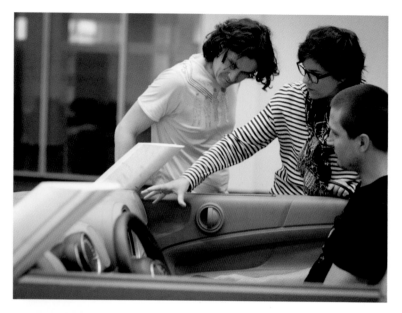

← ↙ ↓ Clay modelling is a skilled task which still plays a vital role in the development of a new car. It's from these models that detailed, three-dimensional digital images will be generated.

steps as the sketches will become full-size, three-dimensional models fashioned from easily worked industrial clay, which are the first time that the designers are able to view them in such a way. This is the point at which a design really comes to life and is an opportunity to refine every single aspect of how the finished MINI might look. But it's not only the appearance that's important, as models like these mean the teams can begin to look at the more tactile elements of a car's design, such as exploring materials and surface textures.

But even at this stage there is still plenty more work to do as the clay models are scanned and enter the computer-aided design (CAD) phase of the project, becoming three-dimensional digital images. These provide designers with almost unlimited scope when it comes to examining the proposed new model in the finest of detail. From the way shapes and colours will work together on the outside in different lights to the appearance and location of switches and dials in the cabin, the ability to view large, high-quality images is an invaluable tool when it comes to the design process. You've probably not spent much time thinking about the location, colour and feel of the interior door handles in your MINI but you can be sure that many hours have been expended on them!

Key steps and timescales

From setting the initial brief to bringing a finished design to market takes around four to five years, but here are the key design stages and timescales within that process:

■ Input is collected. This involves agreeing the proportions; setting a technical framework for the design; obtaining customer feedback undertaking market research to inform the design; defining the character of the car and exploring new technologies – around eight months.
■ Producing sketches and the full size tape drawings. Between four and ten designers

will be working on the exterior and interior sketches. Several reviews ending with final sketch review and the selection of three exterior and three interior sketches by the Head of BMW Group Design – around three months.

■ The clay and digital modelling process. At this stage, three designs are being modelled and the BMW/MINI Board will select two of those for further work and then feedback. Refinement of the clay models and further design and engineering processes. Then selection of the winning models by the BMW/MINI Board – around twelve months.

■ Further refinement of the winning models followed by the BMW/MINI Board confirming the model that will be taken through to production – around ten months.

Revolution or evolution?

The development at MINI has mostly been viewed as an evolutionary process, a logical extension of the historic design language but with contemporary interpretations. All MINIs are characterised by the fact that they provide as much space as possible for the occupants in the smallest possible footprint in order to maximise interior space.

The short overhangs and the principle of 'stance on the wheels' – which means that the four wheels are positioned at the outermost part of the body – underline the sporty character of the MINI. This gives it its distinctive appearance and the typical go-kart driving experience. So even when growing in size, giving a model a makeover or expanding the MINI family, the MINI design concentrates on transferring the typical proportions of the vehicle, the look of the body, the continuous window graphics and roof top, to a new product. The MINI form language is furthermore based on a play of contrasts between basic geometric forms, in general inspired by circles, ellipses, elongated holes and hexagonal shapes.

The design vocabulary contains many traditional and heritage-driven icons. These are a good basis for looking into the future, and in the creative process their form language is constantly interpreted in a modern and innovative way. Certain 'genuine' design icons have been retained from the classic

Mini and have always been developed further – for example the hexagon grille, the round headlamps and the interpretation of the side scuttle including the side markers. In the interior the central display screen, the toggle switches and the door ellipse (the bezel) are further examples of authentic adaptation. At the same time MINI is unique because of its uncompromising combination of rational and unexpected elements, because of its balance between heritage and innovation, because its form shows personality and character and because it is inspiring and rebellious. The MINI design team ensures that the hallmark brand features are regularly revised in keeping with the times and technology, while simultaneously preserving the essential MINI character.

How MINI design has evolved

One of the areas we were keen to explore in this chapter of the manual was how the design of the MINI has evolved. This is what the designers told us:

The exterior

■ Additional edges closely follow the contours of existing elements such as the wheel arches, headlights and rear lights, making the design more prominent and contemporary. This formal echo divides larger sections of the car body and gives the new MINI a more defined character.

■ As a first, the grille of the new MINI Hatch sports a seamless, uninterrupted chrome frame that makes it look even more upscale. At the same time, the hexagonal shape is more clearly recognisable. The grille draws far downward into the front fascia, making the front appear leaner and sportier. The black safety bar is harmoniously integrated into the hexagonal grille together with the number-plate frame.

■ With their signature circular shape and framed by a continuous chrome ring, the headlights of the new MINI clearly build on the family heritage. The headlight inserts have been redesigned and appear particularly structured and clear. The inserts only feature one large, elliptical element, which is surrounded by an LED daylight-driving ring that mirrors the circular shape of the main light.

The interior

- The most striking innovation in the interior is immediately visible once you get inside. To improve readability, all driving-related displays are now situated in the driver's direct field of vision. There is now no longer a 'centre speedo' as it was known. The central feature behind the steering wheel is the instrument cluster with the round analogue speedometer and, slightly behind and to the left of it, the rev counter. The fuel gauge and its vertically aligned LED lights has been placed to the other side of the speedometer. Meanwhile, the circular, centre instrument has been redefined and redesigned as a graphical element that includes entertainment and navigation functions on-screen.

- Even more attention to detail and refinement. Surprising details and features might sometimes be revealed at second glance or discovered over time, for example a pattern in the centre console or the door pockets; or, in the MINI Clubman, the innovative backlit front-door brackets that create an unparalleled, exclusive ambience and innovative effect at night, thanks to different patterns. Also, one trim option shows real aluminium embossed in the style of English tweed cloth.

Prototypes

Regular readers of car magazines will be used to seeing images of forthcoming models that have been disguised while they undergo road testing. It's something that happens at Plant Oxford, where they assign engineers to be in charge of developing bespoke camouflage for each new model. They work in conjunction with the vehicle's designers to erase character lines almost as soon as they are drawn, as it's important both to keep future products secret and to help build anticipation for a new model. The engineers work with the designers from the beginning, to identify key attributes they want to hide, and they develop a package to disguise those areas, but as the car progresses toward production it's important to test it in an increasingly complete form, and it is extensively tested outdoors in public during the later stages of development.

When the new bodywork is fitted the engineers cover it with hard plastic and soft foam, to mask its appearance. Later this has to be peeled off for more realistic testing of things like aerodynamics and wind noise, so at that stage they apply patterned adhesive vinyl to try to fool the eye. Once all of the testing that can be done with the padding attached is complete, the prototype will then be tested with just the patterned vinyl wraps.

The patterns used have evolved over the years, effectively hiding character lines in bodywork. As light and shadows fall on the bodywork, the aim of camouflage is to flatten the appearance so that those character lines disappear. If engineers can hide these lines from the human eye, computer software will also be fooled, making it harder to recognise or recreate a shape using software that can 'strip' the camouflage. However, camouflage also draws attention to cars that could otherwise be overlooked, so the engineers also need to apply some kind of 'mask' to the front and rear ends to further disguise the appearance.

Even if no cameras see the cars and their components, plenty of people may do, which contributes to the problem. While photographers are able to strip away camouflage using software, people who have seen the car or its parts can anonymously coach them through the editing process. Also worth noting is that camouflaging would be easier if it wasn't for the need to test the cooling of the engine and the operation of climate control systems. It's important not to restrict the airflow because that would prevent the powertrain and HVAC (heating, ventilation and air-conditioning) teams from performing the required tests. And with models also featuring

↓ If you see a car like this on the road it's a development model wearing specially designed camouflage to disguise the details of the finished car.

systems such as forward cameras and radars for adaptive cruise control, collision warning and lane-keeping systems, it's important that the camouflage shouldn't interfere with these when they are being tested.

Introducing a new model

Introducing a brand new model to the production process at Plant Oxford is no easy task, and its one that involves a dedicated team whose work begins almost three years before the cars will begin rolling off the assembly line and heading to their new owners. The sheer scale of the work means it's something we can only touch on in this manual, but suffice to say there are plenty of aspects to consider. Here are just some of the stages involved in bringing a new model to production:

- The project team sets targets and milestones for key areas such as the investment required in tooling and robots; whether structural changes will need to be made to the plant; and the requirements for logistics and the supply chain for parts and materials.

- The team includes project integration engineers who will consider how new parts can be integrated into the assembly process, for example how components will arrive on the assembly line and how both robots and workers will actually fit them.

- The process is broken down into modules for each area of the car, *eg* the front end, interior, engines etc. Up to 50 modules could be used, with around a dozen people working on each.

- Those modules will then be brought together into the assembly of a 'virtual' car, which is done on computer and examines every aspect of the build process. The input of lead line workers is crucial when it comes to understanding the fit and functionality of components and ensuring that the process focuses on efficiency and quality that is right first time.

- Once happy with the 'virtual' car, the project could head straight to production or, if the new model is substantially different from one currently produced, into the prototype phase.

- The prototypes – tens to a few hundred cars depending on the project – are hand-

built in Munich. There, they undergo a huge number of processes involving research and development testing and validation of every aspect of the new car, its equipment and options, and the build process itself. Constant refinement is needed to agree the finished product.

- With the prototypes finalised 'series production' is the next step, which sees the process move from Munich to Plant Oxford. The 'Pruefcube' (you can read more about this in Chapter 3) is used to validate the process of assembly, with 'dry builds' undertaken – assembling a complete car but without welding or adhesives. This is all about ensuring the components will fit together as designed.

- 'Pre-series' build is next and perhaps the biggest challenge, as it takes place on the live production line using real processes and equipment. And it has to be done without any interruption to the current models being built. It's no surprise that everyone involved wants to see the very first car made!

- The build is refined and those first cars are audited. Weeks are spent measuring and checking every aspect, from panel gaps and shut-lines to the noise the doors make when closing, the handling, and the sound of the engine. An audit score needs to be achieved, a score that can begin in the hundreds and will need to be whittled down to less than twenty for cars that meet the desired standard ready for the customer to order.

Introduction timeline

- **30 months** – targets, timescales and volumes are agreed. Virtual and concept builds will have begun.
- **26–22 months** – prototype build begins.
- **18 months** – investment is committed for tooling.
- **12 months** – series production begins with 'dry builds' and use of the Pruef Cube.
- **9 months** – pre-series build on the live line. There are four builds, with cars assembled in batches. At this point, validation and refinement begins ready for the live build.
- **45 days** – the sign-off for production and the point at which dealers can begin taking orders for the new car.

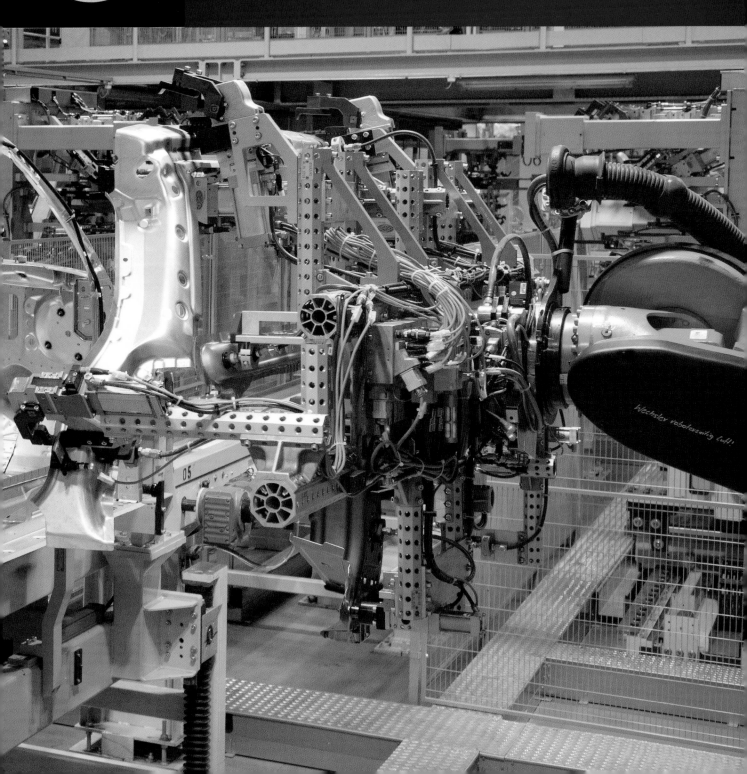

3 Building a MINI

Welcome to the chapter where this manual gets right to the very heart of a MINI – in other words, how it's built. Over the following pages we'll be covering every aspect of how these hugely popular cars are constructed, painted and assembled at Plant Oxford, a site that, as we've already mentioned elsewhere, has a very special place in British motoring history. But it's not just building the cars that happens here, it's also the place that's responsible for such issues as quality control, testing and logistics. This manual will be going behind the scenes in all of those areas and more. But before getting started its worth spending a moment to consider some of the other locations involved in the MINI story.

At present, Plant Oxford is responsible for production of the three-door hatchback models (including the John Cooper Works), five-door hatchback and the Clubman. The Countryman and Convertible models are built at the VDL Nedcar plant in the Netherlands (in July 2014 MINI announced that it would be expanding its production capacity by assembling the hatchback there too). And in Austria there is BMW Plant Steyr, which builds a wide range of engines for BMW models, including the MINI's diesel unit.

In the United Kingdom, though, there are also two further factories that play a key role in the work that takes place at Plant Oxford, one of which is in Swindon, Wiltshire. It's here where body pressings for the MINI are produced, and a place where body production first began way back on New Year's Eve 1955 when it was built by the Pressed Steel Company as an extension of the body-making plant at Cowley. The other important site is the Hams Hall Engine Plant located to the north-west of Birmingham. Once the site of one of the largest electricity-generating power stations in Europe, BMW began construction of the engine factory here in 1998, which was completed at the end of the following year. The first engine was made here in May 2000, with full-scale production getting under way in January 2001. So, both Britain

and Europe clearly have a huge part to play in the MINI story.

And now it's time to start looking at production in a whole lot more detail…

BODY PRESSINGS – PLANT SWINDON

None of what happens in this book would be possible without the work of Plant Swindon, the place where raw steel becomes body panels and parts for the MINI. That steel – which arrives by train at the depot a short distance away from the plant – comes from three main suppliers: Tata steel mills in Europe, including Port Talbot in Wales, and two other suppliers, Arcelor and ThyssenKrupp. About 90% will arrive as huge steel coils (the rest comes as flat sheets), each weighing between 8 and 27 tonnes, and Plant Swindon gets through around 100 coils per week. Not all of it is used for MINIs, though, as the plant also provides panels and pressings – around 40% is exported – for other BMW factories that are building cars on the UKL1 platform shared with the MINI.

After the coils are unwound the first stage in the production process is one of the three 'blanking lines', where either shearing blades or press tools will cut the basic shapes required, using the steel as economically as possible.

→ Rolls of steel, each weighing many tonnes, arrive at Plant Swindon ready to be transformed into MINI panels.

Then the blanks head to one of the 13 'press lines' that will shape the blanks into the finished panels and body sections. The first stage is a draw tool that begins to form the shape while further processes will trim edges, cut holes and fold flanges, depending on the panel being made and its shape and complexity. For example, a bonnet will go through six processes while only four are needed for a door panel or roof (making maximum use of the raw materials, the section cut out of the latter for sunroof-equipped cars is used to make smaller parts).

Facts and figures

- The depot close to Plant Swindon holds an approximately four-week stock of steel. The Swindon plant itself holds only eight hours of stock.
- Each coil of steel weighs between 8 and 27 tonnes. A single lorry delivers each one, which is covered for protection.
- The plant consumes about 100,000 tonnes of steel per annum.
- About 800 tonnes of force is used to cut the steel on the Blanking Line. The coils are unwound at 115m per minute, with feed accuracy of just 0.1mm.
- On the Press Lines, up to 2,000 tonnes of pressure is needed to draw and form the panels and sections.
- The average time to produce a batch of panels is five hours. A batch comprises 1,500–6,000 panels, dependent on line speed and part usage.
- Plant Swindon operates seven days a week, with day, night and weekend shifts. Some of the press lines operate 24 hours a day.
- Approximately 800 people work at Plant Swindon.
- The plant occupies land equivalent to the size of 64 football pitches. Production facilities total 450,000m^2.

- For current MINI and BMW models, the plant produces around 366 types of panel using 880 press tools.
- To produce the completed door, bonnet and tailgate assemblies for MINI (39 different versions), 250 robots are used.
- Assemblies are welded using lasers; each MINI body contains 8.4m of laser weld.
- An average of four days' worth of finished stock is held at the plant. Parts are delivered to Plant Oxford on a 'just-in-time' basis, with 80–90 lorries leaving Swindon every day.

↓ An aerial view of Plant Swindon in Wiltshire.

ROGER NEWMAN

GROUP LEADER FOR QUALITY AND LOGISTICS AT PLANT SWINDON

Roger is a self-confessed petrolhead: 'I was always mechanically-minded at school and built a kit car with my father, so it's perhaps no surprise I've ended up in the motor industry. After taking A-levels an apprenticeship appealed, and being from Swindon and having done some work experience at the plant in its Rover days it seemed the obvious step. I started on a four-year technical apprenticeship back in 1990 and was also sponsored through a degree course, so it was a really solid grounding for the work to come, and definitely something I'd recommend. Early jobs focused on quality in sub-assembly, working with both Rover products and Honda at Swindon, which then led to roles in metrology, quality management in the press shop and project management. Now I've got overall responsibility for quality and logistics at the plant, a job that's both satisfying and challenging in equal measure.'

↑↑ Bonnets being produced on the press line at Plant Swindon.

↑ The completed panels and sections are stored awaiting transport to Plant Oxford; up to 90 trucks depart from Swindon every day.

Quality is crucial, so at the end of the press line parts are carefully inspected, with those destined for outer body sections checked with a highlighting wipe that replicates the paint finish used later. As even the smallest amount of debris trapped in a press tool could cause a defect in panel surfaces – which would require rectification later – these checks are an important part of the process. Inspection passed, the panels are carefully packaged before being sent to Plant Oxford by road.

Recycling

Around 45% of the steel that arrives at Plant Swindon ends up as waste, all of which is sent to a nearby company for recycling. Conveyors under each press line collect the offcuts and send them to a baling machine, each bale weighing around half a tonne. Unusually, a robot is used to carefully place each one in a skip – a quieter method than just dropping them in and therefore much better for employees working nearby!

Assembly

While some panels and sections are sent straight to Plant Oxford to be used in Body in White, Swindon also has an assembly facility that produces complete bonnets, doors and tailgates. In a fully automated process, robots assemble these using laser welding. This makes for a lighter, stronger component that needs less adhesive and is more resistant to moisture ingress. In fact, many of the parts produced at Plant Swindon are handled entirely by robots and won't be touched by workers until they arrive at Body in White.

ENGINES – HAMS HALL ENGINE PLANT

The engine is the very heart of a car, and the three- and four-cylinder petrol units installed beneath the bonnet of a MINI originate not from Plant Oxford but from just under 80 miles away – close to Birmingham, in fact – where you'll find the Hams Hall Engine Plant. Completed at the end of 1999, BMW built its first engine there in May 2000 with full-scale production beginning in January 2001.

Before we get into the detail of what goes on at Hams Hall, it's worth setting out some background to engine production. The process of building an engine begins with the logistics function – the section that receives the order from Plant Oxford up to two days ahead of scheduled car production. The units are built to meet customer demand, with completed units entered into a finished store. When the customer requires the unit it is picked and placed into storage crates (pallets) in a set order and sequenced identically to the Oxford vehicle-build sequence. This ensures that the correct engine is supplied and fitted into its designated vehicle. It's a highly organised process that dovetails with the 'just-in-time' system employed throughout MINI production.

Facts and figures

- The Hams Hall Engine Plant site covers around 85 acres and builds three- and four-cylinder petrol engines for both MINI and BMW models.
- Hams Hall also builds the engines for the innovative BMW i8 plug-in hybrid sports car.
- The plant builds around 1,400 engines per day, with one produced every minute.
- More than four million engines have been made since the plant opened in 2001.
- Annual production of machined engine parts exceeds more than one million.

Just like at Plant Oxford plenty of planning goes into the supply of engines, with parts being ordered from suppliers in line with the build sequence; an impressive system when you consider that Hams Hall has the capacity to build an engine every 60 seconds. And to achieve the desired production rate day after day, month after month and year after year requires an awful lot of advance planning. For instance, a great deal of thought by engineers goes into how the engines are actually built, which includes a focus on reducing stress

⬇ The Hams Hall plant that has been making MINI engines since May 2006. A finished engine rolls off the line every 60 seconds.

on workers, and each assembly station is meticulously planned before being introduced. Virtual assembly techniques for station mock-ups are employed to fine-tune each assembly station and ensure good process design, and any changes to the product or new engine variants are given the same treatment. It's the attention to detail that makes a difference.

With so many engines being produced, Hams Hall is an extremely busy place. In the machining area three shifts operate 24 hours a day between Monday and Friday, with one shift working at night over the weekend. In assembly too, three shifts work between Monday and Friday, as well as one over the weekend.

Machining

This is where engine build begins, using cylinder heads and blocks that are cast at a BMW foundry in Germany with forged crankshafts produced by an external supplier. At this stage the parts are known as 'bought out rough' (BOR) material, with very little machining having taken place. The bulk of that work – the various grinding, milling, turning, drilling and finishing processes that turn the raw material into finished components – takes place at Hams Hall and is a highly automated process. It starts with automated guided vehicles (AGVs) collecting the raw stock from a store and delivering it to the start of the machining process where it is loaded by robot into the first operation. At each process stage the machines identify which derivative of part (three- or four-cylinder) is to be machined and adjusts itself automatically to complete the required process.

Agile and flexible machining centres ensure that machining processes can meet the customers' varying demands whilst still being efficient. In each machining line the final processes are reserved for cleaning and inspection, both of which are also automated. After this the finished machined components are carefully placed by robot into bespoke packaging that maintains the components' cleanliness and protects them from atmospheric contamination, rust and damage. This ensures that the finished parts are delivered to the assembly process in perfect condition ready for use. After final packaging the components are taken via AGV to a small intermediate storage area to await sequencing to the assembly process.

At various stages throughout the machining process components are taken both randomly and at regular intervals for measurement. This ensures that the machining processes are controlled at all times. Results are also analysed by experts to enable early process intervention to ensure component variation is kept to an absolute minimum. It might seem like a straightforward process, but it's worth mentioning the complex support system

JIM EUSTACE

GROUP LEADER FOR PRODUCT AUDIT, PERFORMANCE TEST AND QUALITY STEERING

An Austin Ex-Apprentice, Jim started his career in 1986 working for Austin Rover, later to become Rover Group. Throughout his career Jim has always worked in Powertrain roles.

'After my apprenticeship I took a role in Rover's Powertrain division on the new K Series engine, eventually becoming Production Manager for machining and assembly of the KV6 engine produced – a 2.5-litre V6 unit. After some years I moved to Supplier Quality Management, which led to a move from engine production into gearboxes. The gearbox factory was owned by BMW, machining and assembling gearboxes for the then-new MINI. I was responsible for Supplier Quality Assurance. Inevitably, after some years I found my way to BMW's Engine factory at Hams Hall where I have remained ever since.

Whilst working, I continued my education, completing a Master's Degree in Engineering Business Management in 2006.

My current role is achallenging and satisfying, and requires co-ordination and communication between BMW's Engine manufacturing facilities in Munich, Austria and China.'

that's required to produce so many engines to such exacting standards. And it's not just the automation employed during the build that's impressive; for example, beneath the machining hall is an entire system devoted to managing the coolant used during machining. It needs to be stored, refrigerated, pumped and filtered. Then there's the matter of dealing with all of the metal swarf that's generated. Having been separated into cast iron and aluminium it's spun to remove excess fluid and, with any additional debris removed, is ready for recycling.

Assembly

Engine build starts by first downloading the individual build requirements from the logistics order list. The information required to build the engine is written on to a unique data tag that travels with the engine. At each stage of the assembly process this data tag is read and the relevant information used to configure the engine to the customer requirements. MINI's assembly process aims to be efficient whilst at the same time coping with individual customer demands.

Engine assembly is broken down into process streams, as follows:

- **Cylinder head sub-assembly** – here the head is fitted with parts such as the camshafts and valve train.
- **Short block build** – this is the core of the engine and is where selective assembly is used to match the cylinder block, crankshaft, pistons and connecting rods. Selective assembly supports the precision assembly requirements for each MINI.
- **Main build** – at this stage the cylinder head will be fitted to the block and the engine timing set, before other parts such as the cam cover and some electronic sensors are added.
- **Complete assembly** – here the engine will be fitted with the peripheral parts needed to turn it into a finished unit, for example the inlet and exhaust manifolds, ancillaries and wiring harnesses.
- **Engines are configured to meet the individual build requirements**. To ensure the correct configuration and process efficiency, engine kits are used, meaning no wrong parts can be used and there is no excessive walking to obtain parts. Parts are picked in a kitting

⬆ Manufacturing parts such as the cylinder head is a precision process that uses computer-controlled milling machines for complete accuracy.

⬇ Sub-assembly of the cylinder head is completed by hand, the associate adding numerous parts, including the camshafts and valve train.

↑ **Further assembly processes will see additional components attached, such as fuel and exhaust systems, electrical components, and ancillaries.**

area to create the unique engine kit that will then be sequenced to the assembly line. The kit of parts follows the engine through the individual process stream (one for main build and one for complete assembly).

■ **End function test** – also known as a cold test, every engine will have a short test to ensure it meets the specifications demanded. The test powers the engine and simulates various running conditions to check all the systems are operational and there are no quality concerns – all done without fuel. When the engine has been tested it gets a few more ancillary components before being loaded automatically on to a conveyor that transports the engine to a finished unit store, where it waits to be sequenced and delivered to Oxford. All this can happen, from assembly order to delivery to Oxford, within a two-day window.

Validation and audit

Maintaining quality during the assembly process is vital in ensuring the engine's long-term reliability, and cleanliness plays a key part in that. Any particles or debris introduced during assembly could damage components and compromise the engine's life, so all parts are delivered in carefully designed protective packaging that isn't opened until they are ready for use. For example, a particle size of 500 microns (0.5mm) can influence the performance of an engine. Therefore cleanliness is of great importance during the process. Even the factory building has filtered air pumped into it, providing a positive pressure to keep outside contamination at bay. When someone opens a door to the outside, air flows out of the building, not in. Also, small parts may arrive in sealed bags, whilst bigger metal components get bespoke packaging, some of which has anti-rust protection built in. Some electrical components use packaging that reduces the chances of static electricity causing damage to delicate electronics.

Like the machining process, the assembly process carries out a number of checks to measure the quality of the product. This is known as in-process validation. Checks can range from a simple test of the torque required to turn the base engine, down to the torque of an individual screw. The purpose of these checks is not only to ensure the quality of the

→ **Each engine undergoes testing before being dispatched to Plant Oxford. Quality control and reliability is paramount and data from such tests is carefully scrutinised to eliminate problems.**

product, it also provides data to quality experts who can readily identify any sources of variation, thus continually refining product quality.

If all this wasn't enough, one further test is carried out to ensure product quality, known as product audit. For this, finished engines are redirected randomly to the product audit area, where each is placed into a test rig just as if it was in a vehicle and fired up and put through its paces. Specialists use complex equipment to ascertain the engine's performance and the data is analysed for pass/fail criteria. Any variation in test results is investigated to enable the assembly and machining areas to further improve their processes. For example, vibration is analysed to check for any new sources of noise, even noise that some of us can't hear! Engines can even have a special dye added which, when checked under ultraviolet light, can reveal fluid leaks that would not normally be visible to the human eye.

A number of different tests might be performed. Some engines have a short test lasting four hours while others are run a lot longer to simulate longer-term use by the customer. These engines are subjected to a forensic-style strip-down conducted by skilled auditors where every component has some form of inspection, even down to the torque of every last nut and bolt. A lot can be learned from this process and used to further underpin the quality and performance of the engine. After testing, even the engine oil is analysed by a professional laboratory to look for anything that needs to be investigated. All these tests work together to ensure 'conformity of production'; essentially the information that we read in magazines and manuals, for example the power, torque and fuel consumption figures that are the elements that the customer experiences.

'No fault forward'

Just like at Plant Oxford, Hams Hall operates a system of 'no fault forward', where any problems encountered during assembly are rectified before the build process can continue. As already noted, numerous checks are carried out during assembly, such as tests for leakage of oil or coolant, but should a problem be identified by an employee, a machine, or during in-process validation, then the engine is redirected to the rectification line, where the problem is investigated. Should repairs or component replacement be needed these are carried out by skilled rectifiers before the engine is returned to the build process at the point at which the problem was discovered, so that it is rechecked. Worthy of note is the fact that information on every engine used in a MINI, such as test results and torque settings, is retained, and can be checked should a future failure occur.

PLANT STEYR

Located in the town of Steyr in the area known as Upper Austria, this BMW plant is at the very heart of diesel engine production for the MINI and is the place where all development of the units takes place. The plant now covers 357,000m² and employs more than 4,500 people, with a wide range of diesel and petrol engines for BMW and MINI models, with 1,261,449 built in 2016. The first diesel-powered MINI was the One D, a model that arrived on the market in June 2003 with a 1.4-litre turbocharged four-cylinder unit producing 75bhp. Today, MINIs are powered by a range of diesel engines in three-cylinder 1,496cc and four-cylinder 1,995cc form, with power outputs ranging from 95bhp to 190bhp depending on model. In terms of production, the process for machining, assembling and testing the diesel engines mirrors that used at Hams Hall for petrol engines.

→ The foundry at Landshut in Germany, a place that produces engine parts for MINI and BMW models.

BMW GROUP PLANT LANDSHUT (FOUNDRY)

Chances are that Landshut is a place totally unfamiliar to MINI owners, but in fact every single MINI contains parts that have been made there. How so? Well, Plant Landshut, to give it its proper title, is home to the light metal foundry that amongst other things produces engine cylinder heads and crankcases for the cars made at Oxford. Located in Lower Bavaria, it's been a part of BMW since 1967, when the company bought car maker Hans Glas GmbH, who were best known for producing the Goggomobil microcar that's much sought after by classic car enthusiasts today (although based in Dingolfing, Glas also had a small factory at Landshut). It now covers some 320,000m^2 and is not only one of the most modern facilities of its kind worldwide, it is also the very first zero-emission foundry when it comes to making sand cores for casting. This innovative procedure allows the plant to reduce the emissions from combustion residue by 98% while at the same time increasing the facility's profitability.

Taking into account the components it makes for other BMW models, it's a place that produces over five million castings – totalling 86,000 tonnes in weight – every year. Five different methods are applied in the series production of cast components, the most suitable of which is selected depending on the specific component's design, the technological requirements and the production volume. It's also worth mentioning a particular innovation that the company say is a first for the automotive industry: the wire arc spraying method. Essentially, this sees the cylinder surfaces of all the crankcases coated with a very thin layer of iron particles, which are applied in liquid form. The results are a reduction in fuel consumption and an extended engine life, both of which will be good news for MINI buyers.

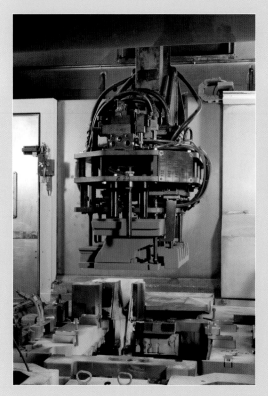

→ Different casting methods are employed depending on the application, but like many aspects of MINI production this is a heavily automated and very precise process.

BODY IN WHITE

Body in White is where the business of building a MINI gets serious – where it's time to turn the detailed planning and the complex collection of parts and materials into the car that you or I might buy in the showroom. It's in this vast area of Plant Oxford that the whole build process begins, and where, over the course of around two and a half hours and at a number of stations, robots will weld, bond and screw the body together with spectacular precision.

The name of this area might stem from motoring history, when the wood used in a vehicle's construction was painted with a white preservative to prevent rot, but today it is a thoroughly modern and highly automated process – around 90% of the tasks are completed without manual intervention – with each operation taking just 60 seconds. And it all starts with the underbody of floor pan, sills and bulkheads before the body sides and roof are added, followed by what are known in this section as 'hang-on' parts – the doors, wings, bonnet and tailgate. Then, after a detailed inspection and cleaning by hand, the finished bodyshell heads off to the Paint Shop for the next stage of the MINI building process.

Sounds simple, doesn't it? Well, the reality is a little more complex, so it's time to take a much closer look at exactly what happens. But first it's worth explaining that the process here

– in the area of the plant known as TR-0-3 – is a little different to that encountered in both the Paint Shop and Fnal Assembly. In fact it's a little more confusing for the visitor, as instead of the car moving through a set of very clearly defined stations, with parts or processes added at each, Body in White essentially starts by constructing a number of sub-assemblies that only later come together to form the finished bodyshell. We will therefore look at each in turn.

However, before doing that, we'll start with a brief explanation of how the build sequence within Body in White operates. Previously, separate lines were used to assemble the bodies of each of the derivatives made at Plant Oxford, with a predetermined number of models built each day. However, this system had a potential weakness in that delays on one particular model

↑ Racks of panels that have arrived from Plant Swindon are stored for just a few hours before being fed into the Plant Oxford production process.

Facts and figures

- ■ This area of the plant covers 100,000m² (or 14 football pitches) and employs 650 people over three shifts.
- ■ Around 1,000 robots are used to weld a finished body, which weighs 350–400kg depending on the model.
- ■ 435 panels are used for each body, with around 80 lorry-loads of parts arriving from the Swindon plant each day.
- ■ Each body contains up to 6,000 spot welds. The temperature at the core of each weld is 1,500°C.
- ■ Each body contains around 60m of bonding seam and up to 8.4m of laser seam welding.

line could mean the Paint Shop, and therefore Final Assembly, received too many types of one model and not enough of another. Therefore since the introduction of the latest 'F56' MINI the plant has operated using the IPSL ('international production system – logistics') method, which means that the electronic 'call' to build a specific car, and the parts and materials required for it, are made together. And it is the order of those 'calls' that sets the build sequence within Body in White, where just four hours' worth of stock is held. Having 250–350 completed bodies held in a store does provide something of a buffer should a problem stop production (remember that with just one line an issue at any stage could stop the whole process), and it's also worth noting that during storage the bodies can be re-sequenced as required by the Paint Shop. Now, on with the build…

Bulkhead

The bulkhead is a significant structural part of every car, not only acting to separate the engine compartment from the passenger cabin but also as a section of the shell to which numerous parts are attached. For example, it's used as the mounting point for the dashboard assembly as well as components such as the pedals and brake servo. And it usually forms one of the

'hard points', the measurements that define a car's shape and dimensions.

For the MINI, the main bulkhead pressing comes from the Swindon plant, and once at Body in White it receives a number of additional parts before it is ready to form part of the bodyshell; these include strengthening brackets and the fitment of studs that will support other components. It's also worth noting that the commonality of parts means that all of the models made at Oxford share the same bulkhead pressing, and one that cleverly incorporates what engineers refer to as 'dual steering pockets'; these mean that the same bulkhead can be used for both right- and left-hand-drive models, reducing complexity. Additional sections include the scuttle panel – the section below the windscreen. These are loaded into a frame ready for welding. Once finished, a robot lifts the bulkhead on to a conveyor where it is transferred to the next main area of assembly.

Front end complete

It's within this robot cell that a number of key sections come together to form the front end of the bodyshell. The main sections are the bulkhead and the left- and right-hand side members, incorporating the suspension turrets.

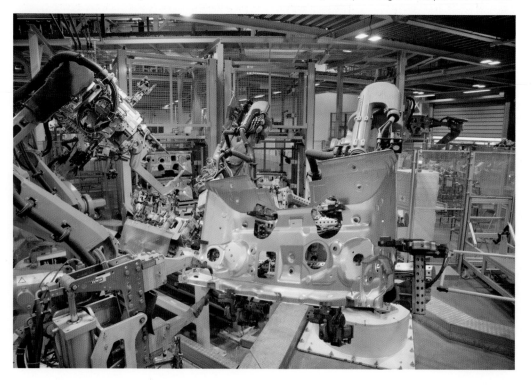

→ Here, the front bulkhead is being constructed. The numerous holes and cut-outs are precisely located, ready to accept components that will be added during final assembly.

But the front end also incorporates a chassis rail that extends rearwards on each side.

Before any welding takes place a robot applies a bead of sealer at various points to help prevent moisture ingress in the future, and then the bulkhead and side members are clamped in a specially designed jig. Accurate alignment is crucial at this stage as the front end not only plays an important part in the overall suspension geometry but also forms the mounting point for the front subframe. Misalignment here would cause significant problems when the powertrain was fitted during Final Assembly, so the jig ensures accuracy to within +/–0.1mm. An ABB robot first makes some crucial spot welds to hold the sections in place and maintain alignment before a further series of spot welds are applied to complete the front end.

Rear end assembly

The process here is essentially similar to that used for 'front end complete'. Once again, the sections – all of which have been pressed at the Swindon plant – are joined together in a dedicated robot cell. The number of sections depends on the model being made, but as an example the rear end of the current 'F54' MINI Clubman comprises eight key parts: the left-

ALEX MCKENZIE

QUALITY SPECIALIST

'I was studying motorsport engineering at Oxford Brookes University and came to the plant as a placement student back in June 2012. Initially here for a year, I was involved in the preliminary work on the F56 three-door MINI and was tasked with defining and introducing an in-line measurement process ahead of production. Basically, that meant translating all the measurements and tolerances from the hand-built pre-production cars into how things would actually fit together when the cars were assembled through normal production. It was fascinating work, with plenty of responsibility and the chance to develop solutions for myself. It turned out that I ended up never leaving MINI, instead spreading the remainder of my degree over three years whilst continuing to work at the plant. At some point in the future I'd like to indulge my passion for motorsport through work, although in what capacity I'm not entirely sure. For now, I thoroughly enjoy my role at Plant Oxford and get my motorsport "fix" through track days and tinkering with cars in my spare time.'

hand and right-hand wheel arches/suspension turrets; boot floor; rear cross-member; seat pan; left-hand and right-hand longitudinal members; and the rear end closing panel (behind the rear bumper). This involves the same sequence of operations as for completion

← The bulkhead becomes part of the 'front-end complete' assembly being welded here, which includes chassis rails and suspension turrets amongst other sections.

SCOOTERS

In a building that covers the same area as 14 football pitches, getting from one end of Body in White to the other can involve plenty of walking. But Plant Oxford has an answer to that potentially tiring problem. Associates can use one of a couple of dozen or so scooters to get around. They were originally intended to help maintenance workers reach a job more quickly, but now anyone needing to get about in the minimum of time can hop on one. Usefully, they even have space to carry tools or small parts.

➜ A number of sections are brought together to form the rear-end assembly being constructed here. It will soon join the floor in the next stage of the process.

of the front end: the application of sealer, the clamping of the sections in a jig for accurate alignment, and spot welding.

The main floor

Obviously a major part of any car, the main floor pressing itself is produced at Swindon; but there is plenty of work to do before it is ready to form the body of a MINI. Despite producing cars that differ notably in length, and that therefore use a specific floor pressing, all are constructed on the same line within Body in White. And one of the first steps for all of them is the addition of strengthening sections, plus brackets and some studs for other components such as the seat belts and seat mounting points. These are followed by the section forming the centre

tunnel, where holes are also made for the gear lever and handbrake that will be added in Final Assembly. Once again, a robot applies sealer where appropriate and all of the spot welds are done by robot, but associates will also load individual parts into a frame ready for welding; applying to a number of processes within Body in White, this is explained in a separate section on page 55.

Underbody geometry

This is the area where the sections mentioned so far come together, and where the bodyshell really begins to take shape. Firstly, the completed front and rear ends arrive at the cell in pairs for the particular model being built. Cameras and sensors mounted on a robot will

→ The beginning of 'front- and rear-end marriage' where the front and rear ends and floor are accurately located prior to welding.

↘ Initial spot welds ensure the correct alignment of the sections before final welding takes place.

↓ Robots deliver the sill section from sub-assembly to the welding cell.

check that the parts are correct – comparing them with the pre-programmed build sequence – before placing them on to a conveyor. The same happens for the main floor section, all three parts mounted on locating pins that will ensure the correct alignment between each section; the front end is positioned first, followed by the floor and the rear end. Then it's on to welding.

A number of crucial spot welds are made first, these ensuring the correct geometry and alignment of the three sections before the remaining strengthening welds are made.

Sills (inner)

Adding further structural integrity to the body, the inner sills are the next sections to be added. The assembled sills are stored in racks, with left- and right-hand sides stored either side of the welding cell. One robot picks up the sill, placing it on a frame above the walkway between cells, while another moves it from there into the welding area. After cameras have checked the parts against predetermined measurements, sealer is applied before the sills are clamped into position and spot-welded to the floor section. This section is also somewhat unusual in that the bodies travel backwards down the line, something that's reversed for later operations.

Underbody studding

With the front and rear ends, floor and sills now completed the underframe heads to one of the six dedicated studding cells to have up to 240 studs attached (depending on the model being built). These small, threaded studs will form the attachment points for the hundreds of components that will be fitted in Final Assembly. As with so many tasks within Body in White, the

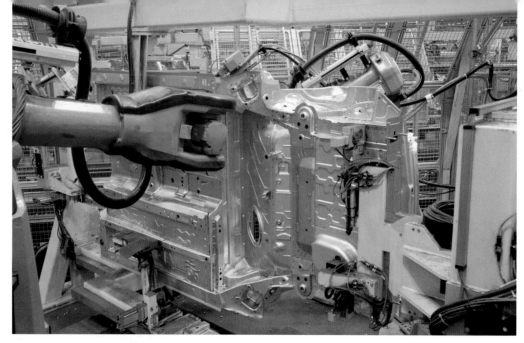

→ The studding cell, where numerous studs are attached, ready to receive the components that will be added during Final Assembly.

↓ In this completely automated process, the studs are stored alongside the cell and fed to the robot head for attachment.

↘ Here, some of the threaded studs that have been welded into position are visible. The image also shows just some of the thousands of spot welds in each MINI.

job is entirely automated. The studs are stored in containers alongside the cell, from where they are fed down a pipe by air pressure to the robot head and resistance-welded into position. The quality and position of the studs is constantly monitored, and should the robot detect any that don't meet the predetermined criteria it will automatically reject and discard them. With all of the studs fitted, the underframe will then continue to a number of further robot cells where additional work takes place.

Framing 1

The side of a MINI – the part forming the door and roof frames and the main pillars – may look like a single section, but is in fact made up of three individual elements. In the area known as Framing 1 there are ten robots whose job is to join the inner frame to the now complete underframe. Each section arrives by conveyor, and, as we saw in the front and rear end marriage, a robot selects the appropriate tool to pick up the correct body side for the model being built. After sealer has been applied, the inner frame is lowered into position beside the underframe, ensuring the correct alignment of the sections prior to welding. The whole assembly then heads to a framing gate where the first spot welds are made to secure the basic dimensional accuracy of the structure; both the left- and right-hand sides are worked on simultaneously.

Framing 1 also sees a number of other parts welded into position, including the header sections above the front and rear screens that join the two sides together, along with roof support spars. The bodies then enter what's known as 'Framing 1 re-spot', where the rest

← One of the operations in 'Framing 1' includes the fitment of drain pipes for models specified with a sunroof.

↓ The bare shell enters 'Framing 2' where the structure will be strengthened by the addition of further panels.

of the welds are added to provide the required structural integrity. The reason that welding is done in two stages is that attempting to complete it all in one stage would exceed the cycle time in earlier areas of Framing 1. In fact, the re-spot area is also where cars equipped with a sunroof have the drain tubes fitted; these rubber pipes, which prevent excess water entering the cabin, are located above the headlining on each side of the vehicle and run within the front and rear screen pillars, draining the water on to the ground.

Framing 2

Where Framing 1 provided the basic shape of the bodyshell, the next area sees further strength added to the body sides. As well as additional spot welds – it's here where the most spot welds are added to the entire body – the

← The body sides are held in specially designed frames before being offered up to the shell. They will be welded into position at the next stage.

↑ One of the incredibly accurate Perceptron cameras being used here to check a bodyshell.

QUALITY CONTROL

Go back to the 1970s and many British cars had a reputation for poor build quality, corrosion and woeful reliability. However, today companies like MINI invest huge amounts of effort and technology in quality control. And at Body in White a system of 'no fault forward' ensures that cars don't continue on the build process until a defect is corrected, rather than waiting until the body is complete.

Key tools in this process are the 'Perceptron' cameras, robot-mounted lasers measuring over 500 points on the body. Accurate to +/−0.05mm (half the width of a human hair), these monitor alignment and dimensional accuracy, checking each body against predetermined values and tolerances and against original build specifications. A number of actions can be triggered depending on the severity of the problem detected; a major variance to expected tolerances could stop the line completely, or the system could just flag a warning, allowing an associate to decide that measurements are still within an acceptable range and allow the build to continue. But while the Perceptron cameras concentrate on dimensional accuracy, other 'vision tools' are employed to check on issues such as the positioning and amount of sealer and adhesive applied to panels, and to ensure that components and processes are correct. This constant monitoring also has another benefit, in that it allows associates to spot trends over a period of time, thereby enabling investigation to take place before a problem becomes more serious.

What visitors will also notice are the calibration posts located at the Perceptron stations. Each post, a couple of feet or so

→ The cameras are checking for any deviation from predetermined tolerances; any problems will be identified immediately.

high, is mounted in a fixed position and has three small, reflective balls on top. As the cameras know what position the balls are expected to be in across three axes, these allow the robots to orientate themselves prior to taking measurements. If a problem is detected, or a scheduled quality check is due, a robot will lift the body from the line and deposit it in a separate area for collection and further examination. And with so many joining techniques used in each body, checking their quality is vital; hence the monitoring of parameters such as current flow for spot welds. Scheduled sampling of completed bodies is also used; a spot weld can be examined using an ultrasound probe to check weld size and depth, while a hammer and chisel can test joints to destruction. Finally, each complete body is cleaned and checked by hand to ensure the surface is free of any defects.

→ Note the different colour metal at the central B-pillar. For safety reasons, a thicker gauge of steel is used here.

↓ The outer body sides about to be fitted at 'Framing 3'. Note the roof appearing from the right corner of the photograph, which is just about to join the shell.

middle frame is fixed into position, a section that includes the B-pillar, which is fashioned from a much thicker gauge of steel. Indeed, it's in Framing 2 where the shell gains much of the strength and integrity that's crucial in protecting occupants in the event of a crash. It's also in this area that numerous metal brackets are attached ready for when the body arrives in Final Assembly, along with foam pads used

both for acoustic reasons and to prevent water ingress. Once welding is completed, all bodies head to 'Framing 2 re-spot' where further strengthening welds are added.

Framing 3

Transported by conveyor from Framing 2, the bodies now arrive at the final framing station. Here, the shell receives the side outer frame

that forms the final surface of panels that will be presented for painting. Once again, a number of smaller parts including brackets and additional metal sections are fitted – although fewer than in previous framing stations – and a robot will select the correct tool for the model being built to pick up and transfer the side to the welding cell. At first it's just held in place against the middle frame by the sealer that's applied, until crucial spot welds are made to ensure the correct geometry. The remaining spot welds complete the job, although it's worth noting that the main strengthening has already taken place in Framing 1 and 2. It's also at this station that the roof is fitted, a robot swinging it into place immediately after the two side frames are positioned.

Auto bolt-on line

Also known as Finish 2 (Finish 1 being a manual process for fitting the rearmost doors to Clubman models, which will be an automated process by the time you read this manual), this is the penultimate part of Body in White and is where all of the remaining outer panels are attached.

After each body has visited a Perceptron cell to check the accuracy of the framing that

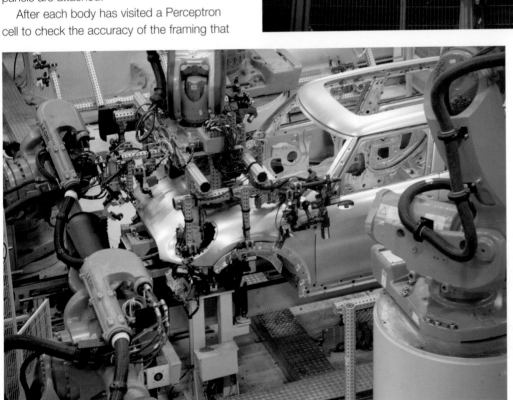

↑ One of the exit lifters that carry completed bodyshells from the framing stations and on to the next part of the Body in White process.

← We've arrived at the 'Auto Bolt-on Line' where components including the bonnet are carefully aligned and fitted.

↑ The doors are fitted to both sides at once in one very quick operation. Here, a five-door model is passing along the line.

↓ A three-door model receives its tailgate. The aperture is laser-measured before fitting to ensure perfect alignment between panel and body.

has taken place so far, they move along a conveyor so that robots can fit the doors, front wings, bonnet and tailgate. First, though, the body is mounted on locating pins to ensure it remains in exactly the right position before a part is fitted, something that also prevents any variation in tolerances between vehicles. Also, each of the parts are fitted using the 'best fit' process whereby cameras simultaneously check the dimensions of both the body and the panel, enabling the robot to position the panel in exactly the right place, taking into account any minor variance in that particular body or panel.

When it comes to attaching the doors, bonnet and tailgate all of the hinges are bolted rather than welded into position, providing a cleaner and less energy-intensive process. The various fixings are stored in containers beside the line and are fed to the robots through pressurised tubes.

The finished body

Having left the auto bolt-on line, the bodies now arrive at the very last part of the Body in White process. Here the first job is to add

← Every completed bodyshell is checked by hand for imperfections, the associates looking for the tiniest blemish that could affect the paint finish.

a fixing for the front wing section located between the front edge of the door and the wheel arch, a task carried out by an associate, who locates a clamp on the A-pillar to hold the wing in place before adding the fixing. Also done by hand is the temporary attachment of a bar that holds the bonnet clear of the wings, something that assists the work of the Paint Shop, along with temporary brackets that hold the doors and tailgate ajar, allowing the protective electrostatic coating to flow into all areas of the body.

An inspection of the surfaces by hand comes next, with any minor defects highlighted for rectification. Then, once the panels have been cleaned to remove any dirt and dust, the

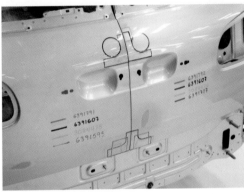

← A reference body – a Clubman model here – highlights areas for particular scrutiny, helping to ensure that every panel is perfectly aligned.

↓ Cleaned and examined, these shells are off to storage ready to embark on the next stage of the build.

bodyshell heads for storage to await its turn in the Paint Shop (approximately 330 finished bodies – the number produced in a single shift – are stored at any one time).

→ Body sections are automatically positioned and rotated in front of a gun that applies adhesive or sealant in precisely measured quantities.

↓ Operations taking place within welding and loading cells are closely monitored and controlled, allowing associates to spot and rectify any problems.

Adhesive and sealer

While the vast majority of the joining processes within Body in White rely on resistance welding (or spot welding, as it's better known), there are areas where adhesives and sealers are used. The former is a type of product used throughout the automotive industry and is applied where extra structural strength is desirable. For a MINI, that means it's used only on the flanges of the longitudinal sections and wheel arches at the rear of the bodyshell. However, the vast number of joints between body and panel sections means that a sealer is also required, used to prevent both moisture ingress and vibration between panels or sections (the latter is why the product is often referred to as being 'anti-flutter', although it does also add some extra strength to the welded flanges). It's also specially formulated (being non-silicone based) so it doesn't cause problems during other processes, for example by reducing the strength and effectiveness of spot welds or contaminating the various protective baths used in the Paint Shop. However, both the adhesive and the sealer are fully cured during the bodyshell's journey through the paint ovens.

Monitoring

While Final Assembly has a dedicated control room that monitors feedback from tools and machinery, the process within Body in White operates slightly differently. Firstly, associates are able to monitor the activity and operations on screens adjacent to each cell or work station, with any problems quickly picked up and notified to the maintenance teams. Every robot and machine is also linked to what's called the IPST (International Production System – Technical) system, which monitors the equipment, feeding back information to a database and producing reports. When a problem is identified, the maintenance teams are automatically informed.

LOAD CELLS

So far we've talked about how the major sections come together in Body in White, but we've not yet addressed how those sections are assembled. For example, parts such as the inner, middle and outer body sides are made up of a number of separate pieces, all of which have to be welded together to form one complete section. And while the majority of the tasks within Body in White are carried out by robots, loading these separate parts into a jig is a job undertaken by skilled associates.

At each of these load cells a screen displays the code number of the vehicle being built – for example, F56 for a three-door car, with F5X denoting a part common to all models – so that the associate knows exactly which parts to select from the racks alongside the station (at this point the order of build has already been sequenced so that completed bodies will arrive in the Paint Shop and Final Assembly in the correct order). With the parts mounted in the correct position on the jig, they are clamped in place to ensure the correct alignment; once the associate has exited the cell and closed the safety shutter the jig rotates, presenting the assembled parts to the robots for welding. With up to four jigs mounted on one turntable, associates can be loading parts for the next vehicle while previous ones are being welded.

Once welding is complete, 'exit lifters' remove the finished section from the load cell and transfer it on to a conveyor for transfer to the next stage.

It's a highly efficient process, and one that's key in ensuring the accurate construction of each and every bodyshell. All of the load cells described above are known as 'closed' cells, which means that safety gates have to be closed to separate the operator from the machinery.

↑ Individual, model-specific sections ready to be loaded into the assembly jigs. The parts seen here are for Clubman and five-door models.

← Parts are securely clamped into the jig to ensure perfect alignment prior to welding.

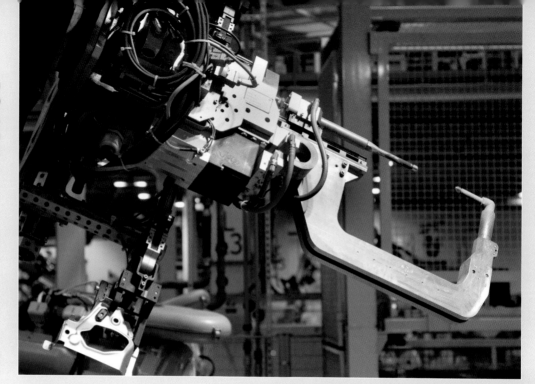

→ One of the welding heads; around 5,000 resistance, or 'spot', welds are made in each MINI.

WELDING CELLS

One of the first things that strikes a visitor to Body in White is the sheer number of robots employed in the build process, and it's likely they'll envision the area to be a sea of sparks as the robots go about the business of welding the bodies together. At Plant Oxford, it's 'resistance welding' (usually known as spot welding) that's used to join the body sections together. This is where a pair of copper electrodes – the welding tips – pass a high current through the pieces to be joined; as the current flows through the metal a resistance is generated that forms a molten pool of metal, which then cools to form the spot weld.

Sparks only occur when the weld tips begin to wear and therefore struggle to deploy the electrical energy needed for welding with the same level of efficiency. Since this could compromise the safety of associates working within the area, technology is on hand to minimise the amount of sparks, which it does in two very clever ways. Firstly, the weld tip is monitored for wear and can be 're-dressed' during production to return it to good condition. However, once a tip has

become too worn for re-dressing the robot can automatically discard it (the old tips are dropped into a plastic bucket and collected for recycling) and select a fresh one from a container within the welding cell. Taking just a few seconds this means there is no delay in production, and the system not only makes for a safer working environment but also helps maintain the quality of the welds.

Should a problem develop that requires an associate to enter a welding cell, then a special key system ensures that when the access gate is opened the cell changes from automated to manual mode. This means it is no longer operating as part of the automatic production process, but allows the associate to operate a robot using a dedicated control unit for diagnostic or repair purposes. An interlock system ensures that the cell can't return to automatic operation while the keys are engaged with the access gate, ensuring safety for any associates working within.

The table provides an estimate of the number of spot welds that go into each version of the MINI built at Plant Oxford:

Model	Front end	Rear end	Main floor	Underframe	Side frame	Framing	Bonnets & doors	Total
3-door	900	1,050	500	400	600	1,350	425	5,225
5-door	900	975	525	400	650	1,475	500	5,425
Clubman	900	1,275	525	425	575	1,450	600	5,800

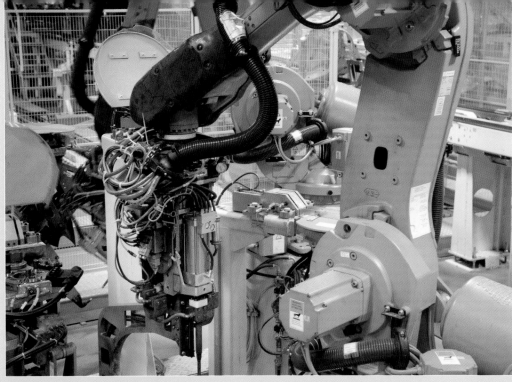

← The robots are programmed to select the correct welding head for a particular task, as well as automatically swapping worn welding tips for fresh ones.

↓ Dedicated welding cells are employed for safety reasons; operations stop if an associate enters the cell using the special access key.

PAINT SHOP

Body in White might be responsible for building the core of a MINI but it's what happens during the next part of the process that will catch the eye of potential customers under the bright lights of their local showroom. Welcome, then, to the Paint Shop, where a MINI gets its final colour, not to mention the extensive protection that will keep its body free from corrosion and environmental damage.

This latter point is an important one, as this stage of the build process is very much focused on longevity. Each new MINI has a 12-year anti-corrosion warranty, so plenty of effort goes into ensuring that rust – once the bane of cars rolling out of British factories – won't be affecting this one. The era of people spraying a car by hand is long gone, for this is now a highly automated process that takes each body through more than a dozen different processes from its very first stages of cleaning and metal protection to that final glossy shine. Mind you, it's not all done by robots; as we'll see, humans bring vital skills and experience to the business of giving every MINI a pristine, blemish-free finish.

It's also worth mentioning an additional challenge faced by the Plant Oxford Paint Shop, and that's the impressive range of colour options that are available. With 16 colours for the body and a further four choices for the contrasting roof, there are hundreds of combinations on offer, which makes the painting of a high volume of cars every hour an even more remarkable achievement.

A particular aspect of the way cars are painted at Plant Oxford is the use of 'body bars'. With each body mounted on two such bars – one at the front and one at the rear – these carry a plate containing information such as the body style and the colour that's been chosen for the body and roof. Read by scanners as the body enters the Paint Shop, that information is relayed to the relevant station so that the car that emerges at the other end is just as the customer wanted.

Witnessing the transformation from bare metal to painted body is fascinating, but it's preparation and cleanliness that is key. So let's take a detailed look at the process, beginning with the paint itself.

↓ **This chart shows the depth of each paint layer in MINI's IPP process compared to a standard four-stage process.**

INTEGRATED PAINT PROCESS

Until 2006 MINIs were painted using the standard process used in most car factories, which involved the application of four main layers. There was an electrostatic coating for protection; a 30-micron primer coat; a 15-micron base colour coat; and finally a 50-micron coat of clear lacquer. But, in a world first, Plant Oxford introduced the 'integrated paint process' (IPP), where the key difference was replacing the primer coat with a 30-micron base coat. Applied in two layers (and wet-on-wet, so there was no drying time between them) the first provided the stone-chip and UV protection properties of the traditional primer while the second gave the colour and depth that buyers admire.

The two main benefits of the new process are an increase in production capacity, as the area used for primer application could now be used as an additional line for applying colour coats without any extra space being required; and IPP is more environmentally friendly, with MINI claiming a 14% reduction in energy consumption and a 13% reduction in the emission of harmful volatile organic compounds, *ie* solvents.

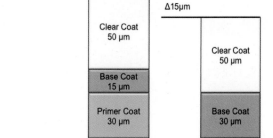

Film Build Comparison: Integrated Paint Process vs. Standard Paint Process

Δ15μm

Standard:
- Clear Coat 50 μm
- Base Coat 15 μm
- Primer Coat 30 μm
- Electro-coat 20 μm

IPP:
- Clear Coat 50 μm
- Base Coat 30 μm
- Electro-coat 20 μm

Transfer Primer Coat functions to Basecoat
- Stone chip resistance
- UV protection

Paint storage and mixing

The paint used on the MINI arrives at Plant Oxford in sealed steel containers known as 'totes'. Each of these totes holds around 1,000kg of paint, which on arrival are sent to the storage room adjacent to the Paint Shop. Although it won't be there for long, care is needed to maintain the paint at a temperature that will ensure it's in peak condition and ready for use. The number of totes used varies depending on the popularity of the colour, but it is quite possible for the Paint Shop to get through somewhere in the region of 10,000kg a month of a popular shade such as Pepper White. And then there's the 'clear coat' that is applied over the top of the colour; this is the lacquer that provides both shine and protection. As this is applied to every car usage is much higher, with around five totes emptied in each seven-day period.

The paint itself needs to be conditioned so that it's at exactly the right viscosity – the thickness of the liquid – for the paint robots, so it will normally be thinned with demineralised water if necessary. Once ready for use, the paint is piped from the tote to a 300-litre 'day

↑ The paint storage room at Plant Oxford ensures the various colours are kept in optimum condition ready for use.

↓ From these 'day tanks' the paint is pumped – via kilometres of pipework – to the robots in the spray booths.

Facts and figures

- The Paint Shop covers an area equal to 17 football pitches, and includes 16km of conveyors and 30km of pipes.
- Around 45 cars leave the Paint Shop for Final Assembly every hour, having been painted by more than 60 robots.
- It takes 4 litres of colour coat to cover a MINI.
- Depending on the model, each car uses 1.6 to 1.9 litres of cavity wax and 77m of seam sealant.
- It takes 9.5 hours to paint a MINI, but 13.5 hours if it has a contrasting roof colour.
- Buyers can choose from 16 body colours and four contrasting roof colours. That's more than 600 variants in total.
- Pepper White is the most popular colour. The next most popular is Midnight Black.

↑ **MINI Plant Oxford's Paint Shop – a labyrinthine building where MINIs take on their colour.**

The bodies are transported to the Paint Shop by an automated conveyor system and embark on a 16-stage process that will see them transformed from basic metal to a glossy finish. The bodyshell that arrives from Body in White carries a protective coating which prevents corrosion forming. However, it's crucial that the body is free of all grease, dirt and other contaminants before the painting process begins.

Known as the deluge, the body is cleaned using process water that removes any large particles of dirt. At a temperature of between 40°–50°C, this stage takes just over 30 seconds and the water is filtered before being reused. Two further stages of cleaning follow – lasting for four minutes – using a mixture of water and alkaline chemicals. Each will remove further layers of contaminants. It's worth pointing out that at each of the stages detailed here the bodyshell is fully submerged in the tanks, with gentle movement of the body and agitation of the fluid preventing air bubbles from forming and ensuring that the cleaning and treatment agents reach every cavity. It's crucial

tank'; there's one tank for the contrasting roof colour and two tanks for the main body colour, and electric pumps send it through many kilometres of pipework to the spraying robots. Indeed, that pipework alone holds around 1,500 litres of paint, which gives some idea of the vast quantities being used on a daily basis.

OSTRICH FEATHERS

↓ **Cleanliness is vital if paint imperfections are to be avoided. The answer at Plant Oxford is to use ostrich feathers...**

Anyone who's tried to paint a car will know that nothing ruins a perfect finish more than dirt and dust being present when the paint is applied, so it's safe to assume that the Paint Shop uses the same level of high technology displayed throughout the rest of the production process when it comes to cleanliness. Well, sort of, because prior to paint being applied the bare shell receives the attention of what workers refer to as 'The Emu'. This is a large roller made up of ostrich feathers – yes, you read that right – as nothing is softer or better at removing debris from the body's surface. Farmed in South Africa, only female ostrich feathers are used, as the quality is higher than male feathers (the females are less likely to fight, causing damage), and only the best Grade One items measuring between 13in and 16in long are used to clean a MINI. Importantly, they don't create any static, and work by retaining loose dirt particles, which are then removed by a vacuum extraction system above the roller. The feathers are changed every six months.

that every inch of metal is treated if a perfect paint finish is to be achieved.

Next come a further two stages of rinsing with process water, a step that takes one and a half minutes, with the water at ambient temperature. This prepares the body for the next stage, which is the application of conditioner. Known as the 'activation' bath, the chemicals used ready the metal for the important next step, which is where the process of protecting the MINI's body really begins, the car spending three minutes in a phosphate tank. Applying a thin layer of zinc phosphate to the metal both prepares the surface for later processes and provides a vital element of corrosion protection for the bare metal. After two separate rinses with process water the body moves on to the 'passivation' tank, where a zirconium-based liquid is used to stop any further phosphate crystals forming on the metal and to ensure a smooth surface.

After a final immersion in demineralised water the body heads for a key layer of protection in the form of the 'electrocoat' (or e-coat), consisting of 78% demineralised water and a mix of solvents, pigments and resin. Underpinning all of the following sealing and painting processes, coating the entire shell with e-coat takes four minutes. To ensure thorough coverage to a thickness of 20 microns the paint is electrically charged by 164 anodes located within the bath; this ensures it adheres to the metal and gets into every cavity. The body then enters a three-stage 'ultrafiltration' process that rinses off and recycles any excess coating. To ensure the continued quality of the e-coating process the contents of the tank are filtered every 15 minutes and replaced completely after three months.

Following a final 30-second rinse with demineralised water the coated body heads to an oven, where it will spend 30 minutes at 180°C to bake the e-coat to a tough finish. Plenty of effort goes into ensuring the e-coating is perfect (air pressure within the Paint Shop is always positive to prevent dirt getting in), because the integrated paint process employed at the plant doesn't use a traditional primer coat, which in turn means any imperfections in the surface will be much more obvious. This is why associates check the finished surface using

gloved hands, feeling for any raised spots or dimples that could have been caused during panel pressing. It's only once the body has passed this inspection that it's sent for cleaning by the ostrich feathers described elsewhere in this section.

Sealing

The way in which a modern monocoque bodyshell, like that used for the MINI, is constructed – from separate panels and sections that are spot-welded together – means that a large number of seams are created between its elements. These are often found within areas such as the closure sections revealed when the doors, bonnet and tailgate are opened, within the wheel arches, and within the interior of the bodyshell. Not only do the seams look unsightly, but it's also important to ensure that no moisture can enter them, as this would almost certainly lead to corrosion. The solution is to apply a layer of PVC sealant, which is where the plant's seam-sealing lines come in.

Before that process can begin a number of fittings are screwed on to the bonnet, tailgate and doors; these 'hooks' will enable specific robots to open these sections so that the robots applying the sealant can gain access. Made by Swiss company ABB, the main body of the seven-axis robot has a fabric covering to prevent excess sealant from entering its moving parts, and during operation it is vision-guided,

↑ A MINI body undergoing one of the many cleaning and protection processes employed before the final paint finish is applied.

RACHEL NEARY

PRODUCTION STEERING SPECIALIST

'I always knew I wanted to work in the automotive industry, as my family are in the business and I have long had a fascination with cars. I studied physics at university, which has a very close relationship with engineering in wanting to understand how things work and why, so joining MINI's graduate scheme after my degree was the perfect choice. I was also keen to travel and see more of BMW and so I really enjoyed the chance to spend a year on placement in Germany, working both at the FIZ (Research & Innovation Centre) in Munich, and at the home of BMW "i" production in Leipzig. My current role in Painted Body brings a lot of variety and is integral to how the plant runs. It's really important to me to retain a real connection with the cars, as that's what I enjoy most; in the future I'll definitely look to develop on this within the production and engineering fields.'

↑↑ **A system of 'vision' cameras ensure that sealant is applied in exactly the right locations. Fabric covers prevent material from entering the robot's moving parts.**

↑ **Some areas are too difficult for even the robots to reach, which is where skilled associates come in.**

using cameras. These cameras take references from 'absolute points' – four holes in the bodyshell that act as datums and are specific to each body style produced at Plant Oxford. Once the cameras have located the holes, the robot will know which body it is dealing with and will apply the sealant according to pre-programmed movements across three axes. In addition, some sealant is applied by hand in areas that prove too difficult for even these clever robots to reach.

The next stage of the process is for associates to apply sound-deadening bitumen panels to strategic areas of the bodyshell such as the floor pan, transmission tunnel, and within the doors. Self-adhesive, these are specially cut to shape depending on their position, the lightweight pieces reducing noise and the 'drumming' effect of the flat metal panels, both of which would harm refinement on the road.

Once the body has passed through the ovens employed later in the process, the sound-deadening panels will have been baked firmly into place.

We then come to the final part of this process, which is the application of the traditional underseal. Used on cars for many years, applying the material to the underside of the floor pan and other vulnerable areas protects the body from damage caused by stone chips and road debris, and plays a key role in preventing corrosion. The PVC material is applied by robots, and once cured in the ovens will retain a rubbery finish for extra damage resistance. But, as in many areas of Plant Oxford's operation, this process is designed to minimise waste, so certain areas of the underside – such as those covered by the fuel tank and exhaust system – won't have underseal applied.

↑ Associates apply self-adhesive sound-deadening panels to strategic areas of the bodyshell. Their job is to prevent unwanted noise from spoiling the driving experience.

← The application of PVC underseal protects the vulnerable underbody from stone chips that could cause corrosion later in the car's life.

↑ **A fully protected body just about to enter the spray booth.**

TOM BENNETT

GROUP LEADER, PAINT SHOP

Tom was interviewed in early 2017 before he retired after 38 years' service in the paint shop. He was presented with a model MINI with a goodbye message on a plaque from all at Plant Oxford.

'I've been here since 1978, when Cowley was building cars like the Austin Princess and MGs, and actually painted the very last MGB GT made. It was all a bit different in those days, mind, as we were spraying lead-based paint by hand with hardly any safety gear. No air-fed masks or anything, just a basic facemask, and we used Vaseline to plug the gaps and catch the worst of the spray! It was hot work too, and we even had to take salt tablets because of dehydration. Unbelievable really. Things are very different now, though, and having seen

all the changes over the years I can honestly say that the materials and systems we are using in the plant today are world class. Anyway, I've got a really strong history here as my dad was a foreman in the press shop, working here for 41 years, and my sister and brother have worked here too. And now my two sons are here, one in logistics and the other involved in prepping show cars. I got into line management when BMW took over and have managed in every area of the Paint Shop since. This plant has been my life and I'll be incredibly sad when it's time to leave.'

It's only after all of the carefully designed processes outlined so far have been completed and thoroughly checked that the body will head for the three lines that apply the customer's chosen colour.

The first step on each of those lines is the application of the base coat in one of the 16 colours currently offered by MINI. The first stage is the spraying, by robot, of the areas exposed – the 'shuts' – when the bonnet, tailgate or doors are opened. Remember the hooks that were attached at the beginning of the sealing process? Well, these come into action now as a robot designed specifically for the job will open each of these panels so that the paint can be applied. Then it's on to the rest of the car, where the paint is applied electrostatically, a process in which the paint is effectively drawn to the metalwork to create an even finish. Being water based, it isn't possible to electrically charge the paint itself so that job falls to a number of 'fingers' mounted on the spraying head. These electrodes charge the paint – to around 70,000V – after it's been atomised, and each robot will cover the body in paint to a depth of around 25 microns.

While solid colours will receive a single application of paint, there's a difference when it comes to the metallic shades. These are applied in two stages (wet-on-wet, so with no drying time between applications), the first being the electrostatic application of base coat – 70% of the amount used for a solid colour – with a second spray booth applying the remaining 30% of the mica paint that provides the metallic finish, to a depth of around 15 microns. This latter coat is applied using the traditional method of air pressure to force paint from the gun, a system that produces a much greater volume of excess spray. Indeed, observe the process for yourself and the amount of spray generated is immediately noticeable, which is why the booths utilise a system whereby air units in the roof push air downwards while a water trough beneath the car draws the excess paint down into coagulation tanks. Here the water component and paint are separated for further treatment.

With the base coat applied each body passes through an infrared oven (known as an

← These robots are spraying inside the door shuts, ensuring that every inch of the body is covered.

↙ Painting is almost complete here. Note how the robot at the top of the picture is using the hook fitted earlier to hold the bonnet open.

↙↙ Robots will open the doors, bonnet, and tailgate prior to painting. Here, you can see the hook located at the base of the tailgate that will be used to lift it open.

↓ This image shows the 'fingers' on the spraying head that electrically charge the paint prior to application.

→ The body will pass through a number of ovens during the painting process, each contributing to the glossy and durable finish that customers expect.

↓ An associate checks a painted Clubman body. Plenty of experience and a delicate touch are required, as only perfection will do.

↘ Should a mark or blemish be detected, skilled associates are on hand to rectify the problem before the body progresses any further.

'inter-coat flash-off oven'), which operates at around 80°C. This is a vital step, which is used to drive out moisture from the waterborne paint and prepares the body for the solvent-borne clear coat. Although it leaves the paint looking dull in appearance, failure to do this would run the risk of pinholes and craters appearing in the surface, ruining the final finish. It's also at this stage that lasers monitor each body, checking that the correct depth of paint is being applied.

With the base coat prepared and dry, the body passes to the booths and robots that will apply the clear coat, the layer of lacquer approximately 40 microns in depth that will provide the final protection and lustrous shine that customers expect. Once again all the

spraying is by robot, although the key difference here is that, being solvent-based, the clear coat itself can be electrostatically charged prior to application, once again ensuring that a thoroughly even coat is applied. Then it's back to the oven for 45 minutes, which includes a stoving schedule of 20 minutes at 140°C.

Paint inspection

While all the hard work might have been done there remains one final and very important part of the painting process, and that's a quality inspection. MINI's ethos of striving for absolute quality is mentioned several times in this manual, and it's something that certainly applies in the Paint Shop. And for each MINI

that means a careful inspection by hand, with skilled associates checking every inch of the paintwork looking for minor marks and blemishes. If any are found, a small, hand-held electric polisher is used to remove the mark, although even this process isn't quite as straightforward as you might expect, because each tool is programmed so that the polishing procedure takes exactly 12 seconds – the operator just has to keep their finger on the trigger until the polisher stops – and the timing is monitored and the information fed back to a central database to ensure that the procedures are being carried out correctly. However, the experience of the operators means that some leeway is allowed if they judge a shorter time to be required to remove a particular mark. It's yet another example of the attention to detail employed in producing the modern MINI.

Colour changes

We've already mentioned the numerous colour combinations that can be chosen by the customer, and that could easily present a potential headache for the Paint Shop when it comes to painting somewhere in the region of 1,000 bodies a day (this number can be a little higher or lower depending on the daily target). In order to make the painting process as efficient as possible the main aim is to spray in batches, ie a number of bodies all in the same colour, but where this isn't possible the robots have the ability to spray each body travelling down the line in a different colour (something associates refer to as painting 'Smarties', as in lots of different colours).

Not only is this some feat given the proximity of the bodies, and therefore the potential for overspray affecting the bodies either side – a problem avoided by the exact application process and efficient ventilation system – but a robot changing the colour doesn't even stop the line. Essentially the paint is held in a colour changer unit that pipes the paint to the robot. Should a new colour be required, this unit stops the flow of paint, flushes the pipe and spraying head through with solvent (mainly demineralised water) and then begins delivery of the next colour. It's certainly clever, but as each flush uses around

half a litre of solvent it's easy to appreciate why batch-spraying is preferred.

The contrast roof

Personalisation is a major part of the MINI buying experience, and one of the customer choices is to have the roof painted in a different colour to the body. So how does such a busy paint shop cope with these demands?

The first thing to note is that models configured this way are the only ones to get a second coat of paint; there's just a single application of base coat, remember, which would have covered the whole car. After passing through the final paint ovens, models destined for a new roof colour are diverted to a separate line where associates start by rubbing the roof with an abrasive pad – this provides a 'key' to help the fresh paint adhere. They then mask the rest of the car with plastic sheeting and tape, leaving only the roof exposed, a remarkably quick process that's carried out on a large number of cars every hour. In fact, there's the capability to do this on up to 80% of the daily volume of cars (as noted previously, that volume can be in the region of 1,000 bodies). Then it's back through the spray booth for the new colour to be applied by robot and another trip through the oven for curing. In all, the extra processes required mean that a car with a contrast roof takes around three hours longer to paint than one without.

On a similar subject, buyers can also choose to have their MINI personalised with bonnet stripes and roof graphics. The former are applied by hand in the Final Assembly area,

↑ If a contrasting roof colour has been specified, the main body is expertly masked prior to a further trip through the spray booth.

An associate injects protective wax into body cavities. This is a crucial part of the anti-corrosion process employed at Plant Oxford.

after the completed car has been driven from the line, while the latter are applied by the local MINI dealership.

Cavity wax and foam

Before the painted bodyshells head over to Final Assembly to be turned into finished MINIs, there's an important part of the process that we've not yet explored. Improving refinement and minimising the risk of corrosion is a key consideration in building a modern car, which is why each body travels across an internal bridge to an area that will fill the numerous cavities with foam and wax. It's the former that happens first, an ABB robot injecting around half a litre of foam into areas such as the bulkhead and foot wells; this is an acoustic foam, consisting of a mixture of liquid isocyanate and a chemical called polyol. The body then moves to a separate line where associates use a special air gun to inject a specific quantity of wax into all of the cavities that might harbour moisture and corrosion. Areas such as the bonnet, doors, tailgate, sills, wheel arches and floor pan all get the wax treatment. The last step is for the body to enter the tilt station, where it is rolled gently from side to side to ensure that the wax is evenly distributed.

Painting of plastic parts

Go back a few decades and the business of painting new cars used to be much simpler. One of the reasons is that most of the exterior

parts, such as bumpers, were made of metal (usually chromed) and simply bolted on with no painting required. But as these were steadily replaced by one-piece plastic bumpers that were often colour-coded to the rest of the bodywork, car factories often struggled when it came to ensuring that the colour matched that of adjacent panels. To avoid this problem with the MINI's front and rear bumpers, the facility at Banbury that manufactures them is supplied with exactly the same batches of paint as are delivered to Plant Oxford. That way minor variations are avoided, ensuring a colour match as near to perfect as possible.

Paint Shop monitoring

With so many bodies flowing through the Paint Shop every day it's no surprise to find that its operations are carefully monitored. A dedicated control room keeps track of every car, with associates able to identify where it is in the process and what work has been carried out so far. The monitoring system also receives input from robots that measure the thickness of the paint being applied (the 'film build', as it's referred to). The application and depth of the base coat is checked on every bodyshell, while a sample of finished cars and colours is also checked. The system automatically flags any results that are considered sub-standard so that further investigation can be undertaken where necessary.

← Every aspect of the paint process is carefully monitored and controlled. Associates know exactly where in the process each individual car is at any one moment.

CURRENT PAINT COLOURS

At the time of writing this manual, buyers could choose to have their MINI painted in one of 16 colours (some of which are illustrated in the MINI graphic below). Depending on model and trim level, these are:

Solid colours
Pepper White
Chili Red
Lapisluxury Blue
Volcanic Orange
Rebel Green

Metallic colours
Deep Blue
Midnight Black
Thunder Grey
Electric Blue
Blazing Red
British Racing Green
Moonwalk Grey
Melting Silver
White Silver
Pure Burgundy
Digital Blue

Contrasting roof colours
Black
White
Silver
Chili Red

EXTERIOR COLOURS.
WHICH ONE'S YOURS?

Electric Blue[*,†]

Deep Blue[*,1]

MINI Yours Lapisluxury Blue

British Racing Green[*]

Pepper White[2]

White Silver[*,3]

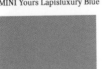
Melting Silver[*]

Moonwalk Grey[*]

Thunder Grey[*,4]

Midnight Black[*,5]

Volcanic Orange[*]

Chili Red[6]

Blazing Red[*,1]

[*] Metallic
[†] John Cooper Works models in these colours are not available with roof and mirror caps in red or with John Cooper Works bonnet stripes.
[1] Not available on John Cooper Works models or with John Cooper Works Chili Pack.
[2] Not available with roof and mirror caps in Aspen White.
[3] Not available with roof in body colour.
[4] Only available on Cooper S/SD and John Cooper Works models.
[5] Not available with roof and mirror caps in Jet Black.
[6] Only available on John Cooper Works models or with John Cooper Works Chili Pack.

Roof and exterior mirror caps.

Aspen White

Jet Black

Body colour

ASSEMBLY

Think of any modern car factory and the chances are that the picture that forms in your mind is of the assembly line, the place where rows of cars inch along as workers attach all the parts necessary to produce a finished car. And that's exactly the stage we have reached with this manual.

Just as with all of the other areas of Plant Oxford that we've visited so far, it's an amazing place, a quietly choreographed hive of activity where some 700 people unite the painted bodyshell with the 3,000 or so parts that will turn it into a finished MINI. Some of those parts, such as bumpers, engines, seats and dashboards, arrive on the line as pre-assembled units ready for installation, while others, from sound insulation to glass, are added at individual stations, either by robots or by hand. Indeed, the system of pre-assembly is an important one when considering the way in which assembly is structured. Having potentially complex sub-assemblies arrive from elsewhere in the plant has a number of benefits, including a reduction in the workload on the main assembly line; the ability to design a more ergonomic workspace with fewer processes taking place; and reducing complexity when it comes to large fitted items such as the dashboard, which helps eliminate the risk of mistakes or damage.

In this section of the manual we'll be taking a detailed look not only at the assembly process itself but at the vast range of activities required to ensure this process happens smoothly for 22 hours a day every day. It's time to see how a MINI finally comes together.

Stage 1

We begin, logically enough, at the very start of the Final Assembly process where cars have arrived from the painted body store, an area that typically holds between 250 and 550 bodies. Arriving on a conveyor with absolutely no parts fitted at all, the first task is to re-sequence the cars from the order in which they were painted to the order already programmed for Final Assembly. Remember, this is now a specific customer car with an order number assigned that designates its final specification from the many options available. That order will have been received approximately a week before assembly begins – the same point at which suppliers receive automatic notification, via the logistics system, of the parts that will be required. With the assembly sequence set, the car is now at the stage known as 'the freeze', when no specification changes can be made by the customer.

Before heading into assembly proper, there are some initial tasks to carry out. Cars equipped with a sunroof need to have a weather seal fitted around the aperture, and those models to be fitted with roof bars (for roof racks and the like) will pass into a laser cell for the mounting holes to be cut. Called 'late-configuring', this reduces the complexity of the body types by not having to produce an entirely separate roof panel.

A cleverly designed 'gullwing' system lifts the cars from the conveyor and on to wooden floor sections known as skillets. Rather than a continuous track as you might expect, there is one skillet for each car, pushed along the line by the one behind. And sitting on top of the skillet is a flexi-lift that adjusts the height of the vehicle depending on the operation being carried out.

GREG DENTON

GENERAL MANAGER, MAIN ASSEMBLY

Greg's story began back in the Rover days: 'I started at the plant in 1992, joining as an apprentice straight from school. As a "business technician" I specialised in logistics, and after completing the four-year apprenticeship spent 16 years in that side of things, including work on the scheduling of materials for use in assembly as well as production planning. But I was ready for something different, something more people – and management – oriented, so I moved across into assembly. It's slightly unusual, moving from a back-line to a front-line role, but I really enjoy working with colleagues here and it's hugely rewarding to see them develop in their jobs.' Asked what the best things were about working at Plant Oxford, he said: 'It's the enjoyment and pride in making such a great product, and also the people. Over 4,000 work here, but we've had 17,000 attend a staff open day – that tells you how proud we all are to show friends and family what we do.'

The operations that come next begin with the removal of the bars applied for the Paint Shop robots to open the doors etc. Gas struts for the bonnet and tailgate are fitted; the Vehicle Identification Number (VIN) is stamped on to the front suspension turret; some under-bonnet bracketry is fitted; and the rearmost doors of Clubman models are removed. It's at this stage that an associate uses a hand-held electric tool to cut a hole in the bulkhead for the steering column, for left- or right-hand drive as appropriate.

Stage 2

With good access needed to all parts of the vehicle, all the doors are now removed. Unbolted by hand, an electric/pneumatic assistor moves them to a conveyor where they are sent upstairs for assembly, a process we'll be returning to later. Beside the assembly line is the area where the sheet of VIN labels is printed and the keys are programmed. Both will travel with the car in a plastic container, with the labels applied at various stages of the assembly process.

Stage 3

The weather seals for the door and tailgate apertures are fitted using the 'scoffing' process, where an air-driven hand tool is

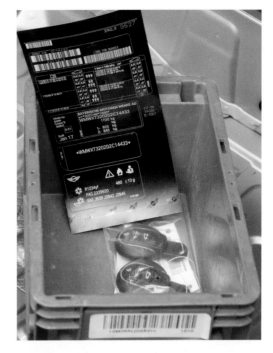

used to compress the metal strip within the seal, ensuring a tight grip on the body flange. The insulation panel for the inside of the front bulkhead is fitted and held in place with plastic clips, and protective rubber mats are applied to the front and rear wings to prevent paintwork damage as the car progresses through assembly. The cars are now ready to be transferred, via a complex

← One of the very first steps in Final Assembly is uniting a car with its VIN labels and pre-programmed keys. They'll travel with the car throughout the assembly process.

↙ Weather seals await fitting. Positioned within easy reach of associates…

↓ …they are expertly located on the body using a special tool.

↑ These rotating slings make the job of attaching components to the underside much easier for the associates, reducing the need to stretch.

ERGONOMICS

Building cars used to be a physically demanding activity, one that involved workers wrestling with heavy parts and machinery, and fitting components in awkward-to-reach places. Today at Plant Oxford there's a much greater emphasis on ergonomics, making the lives of workers a great deal easier, and it's achieved in a number of ways. Firstly, the working environment is brightly lit and much quieter, using electric rather than noisy pneumatic tools. In addition the use of sub-assemblies, such as the dashboard, reduces the need for associates to assemble parts in confined spaces. Handling devices assist in moving parts weighing more than 8kg into position and rotary slings can rotate the entire car 90° depending on the operation to be performed, which means that components can be fixed to the roof and underside with ease.

Having the associates move on a travelling conveyor as they attach parts is safer and avoids unnecessary walking between vehicles. For the same reason, Final Assembly also makes use of small, specially designed carts that hold components and tools and can be pushed or pulled along with the vehicle being worked on; a system suggested by associates, it's another example of trying to make the assembly process as efficient as possible. Adjustable 'flexi-lifts' (mounted on wooden skillets) ensure the car is at exactly the right height for a particular operation, while special rubber flooring helps avoid stress on the joints of associates on their feet for an entire shift. Finally, as an example of continuous improvement, the door assembly line within Final Assembly has been fitted with a moving track; using the latest technology, it features small conveyor modules that take up little space on the plant floor.

↖ The small cart seen here ensures that components and tools are within easy reach; crucial when there is barely a minute for each operation.

← One of the height-adjustable flexi-lifts employed to make assembly operations less physically demanding on associates.

Facts and figures

- Assembly is split into two levels. The main line is on ground level with door assembly taking place on the upper level.
- 1,000 cars roll off the assembly line every day.
- It takes 5.5 hours to assemble each car, with an average of 3,000 parts used depending on the model.
- The assembly line is 1.7km long.
- Around 500 people work on the line during a shift.
- 67 seconds is allotted for each task on the assembly line.

series of exit lifters, to ground level where assembly continues.

Door assembly line

Taking a break from Final Assembly, it's time to detail the process of door assembly, which sees up to 130 individual parts fitted to each door before they return to the main assembly line in exactly the right sequence to meet the correct car. With the doors mounted on a frame, all of the work here is done by hand, with the process being as follows (overleaf):

(It's worth noting that left-hand and right-hand doors are assembled simultaneously, and as with other stations within assembly the parts are located at exactly the right point for each operation, maximising efficiency for associates. However, regular deliveries by lift are required due to the limited storage space on the door assembly line.)

↑ The insulation panel for the front bulkhead is clipped into place; its job is to reduce engine noise entering the cabin.

← First step on the door assembly line is the fitting of weather strips and seals, along with the numerous clips to which other components will be attached.

↖ The electric window regulator mechanism is inserted into the door and bolted into place…

↑ …and then it's the fitment of the exterior and interior door handle mechanisms, the locks and latches, and the cables that connect them all.

← The wiring harness is fed into the door and clipped into place, and electrical connections made for items such as the electric windows and central locking.

↙ The glass is slid into place, fitted from above through the aperture in the door frame, and attached to the regulator.

↓ The waterproof inner door membrane is fixed in place with a pre-applied butyl seal, and the speakers are connected and screwed into position.

↑ The exterior door mirrors are fitted.

↗ The electrical wiring and release cables for the inner door handles are connected to the door card.

→ The door cards – which are manufactured in Birmingham – are clipped into place.

↓ With an electrical power supply connected to the door's wiring multi-plug a pre-programmed test routine checks all of the operations such as those for the windows and central locking.

↘ The door is finished and on its way to re-join the car later in Final Assembly.

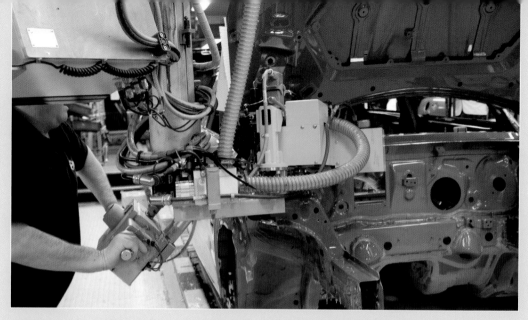

→ An associate engraves the unique iGEF number on to the front suspension turret.

TRANSPONDER AND IDENTIFICATION/TRACKING

↓ A transponder mounted on the bonnet contains all of the customer order data. It will be read at each station to ensure the correct build specification.

↘ A paper form acts as a visual back-up, containing the same data as the transponder.

When you're building 1,000 cars a day keeping track of each one is a huge logistical challenge. Fortunately, Plant Oxford have systems in place to ensure that every MINI is built correctly and reaches the customer with exactly the right specification. That process starts in Body in White, when each shell is assigned a unique 'iGEF' number, a special code that is engraved on to the front suspension turret of the body as a two-dimensional dot-matrix. This identifies the model type and whether, for example, it is to have a sunroof or not, enabling each bodyshell to be traced during the build process.

By the time a car is ready for assembly things have become more complicated still. It's here where each MINI is built to order, incorporating all of the specifications and customisation chosen by the customer. And there is a huge amount of choice! Hence the

attachment of a transponder, a small box containing all of the relevant customer data in electronic form, which is placed on the bonnet of the car and stays with it throughout assembly. Read by sensors at each station, it displays information on a line-side screen so that associates know exactly which parts need to be fitted. It also communicates with the robots to identify which car they are working on and to ensure that the correct sub-assemblies – such as doors – are reunited with the right car.

This complex system also means that every MINI has a record of what parts were fitted and even who worked on the car. This information is stored for ten years. And, just in case, the transponder is backed up by a conventional paper order form that's attached to the underside of the bonnet.

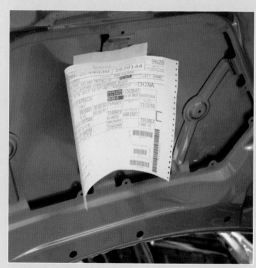

← Here, the sunroof is being fitted. The fully automated operation positions the unit and fixes it into place.

Stage 4

We're back downstairs in the assembly building now, and in a specially darkened area. The reason for the low light is because a camera array is taking a picture of each car, looking for those that have an aperture for a sunroof. Cars without continue on their way to the next process, but when the camera identifies a car that's to have a sunroof fitted it stops in the station and the installation robot collects the sunroof – a fully assembled unit or 'cassette' complete with glass panels and the securing screws – from the stock beside the line. Swinging into place above the car, an upper arm holds the sunroof panel ready to lower it into position while the lower arm enters through the windscreen aperture and fixes the cassette into position from below.

All cars now head on to the next station, one where a raft of smaller parts such as clips and brackets are fixed to the body ready for the fitting of components later in the assembly process. It's also at this stage that the cars are fitted with items such as the washer jet nozzles, pieces of decorative chrome trim and latches for the bonnet and tailgate. Also fixed into place are the side curtain airbag units, mounted along the edges of the roof above the side pillars. And lastly, non-sunroof models receive an important piece of additional sound-deadening in the form of a sheet of cardboard; it might seem a cheap and simple solution in such a high-tech factory, but it's still an excellent insulator. A robot picks up each sheet, applies a layer of adhesive, and then transfers it to an assistor that enters the car

and pushes the cardboard on to the underside of the roof panel, holding it in place for a few seconds while the glue dries.

Stage 5

The next stage of assembly is a vital one: the installation of the wiring harness that will supply power to all of the finished MINI's systems and equipment. The harness itself arrives on a just-in-time basis from the supplier (German company, Draxelmaier) encased in a canvas bag – each harness specific to the car being assembled, which may have a number of optional extras – and the first step is to warm it up. Why? Well, the harness of a MINI is a bulky piece of kit weighing approximately 20kg and containing up to 3km

↓ A cardboard roof insulation panel is fitted into position, but only to cars without a sunroof of course!

→ The complete electrical harness of a MINI, showing the many electrical connections throughout the car.

↓ Each wiring harness is warmed before fitting, making it more flexible and easier to route.

of wiring, not to mention some 500 connections, and when it's cold it becomes much less flexible, and therefore harder to install. After scanning to ensure it's correct for the next vehicle on the line, the harness takes a short trip – still in its bag – through an oven for approximately 20 minutes at a temperature of 25°C before being carefully unpacked and threaded into position within the cabin.

Raised on the skillet's flexi-lift for ease of access, three or four people will normally fit the harness, a process that takes a couple of days to learn; it's all done within the 67-second cycle time, and with 1,000 cars built per day the associates are making some half a million electrical connections each day!

As the car moves through this stage it will be fitted with a number of brackets for interior and exterior trim; brackets for the bumper mouldings; heat shields; and the bonnet release cable. If chosen by the customer the tow bar bracket will also be fitted here. After this comes the carpet, a one-piece item that's fitted not only quickly but accurately too, as wiring connectors must be pulled through pre-cut slots. Next comes the installation of components such as the brake servo, electronic control units (ECUs),

← The associates have just minutes to secure the wiring harness and make dozens of electrical connections.

→ Two associates fit the carpet, ensuring that electrical connectors are fed through for the equipment to be fitted later.

foot pedals and seat belts. It's also here that Clubman models are fitted with their combined rear spoiler/high-level brake light unit.

We now come to a key component in any car – the dashboard. Referred to as the cockpit assembly, it has already been constructed elsewhere in Plant Oxford and arrives at the line in sequence courtesy of an AGV. Lifted from the AGV by an assistor unit, the associate swings the cockpit into place through the right-hand door aperture and bolts it into position. With the electrical harness connected it's on to the next step, where a kit of parts is assembled for each car, containing components such as the distinctive central display screen, in-car entertainment unit and dashboard air vents.

→ Parts – such as these brake servos – are located within easy reach of associates working on the assembly line.

↓ The pedals are fitted next. Here, the associate is attaching the brake and clutch pedals, to be followed by the throttle.

↘ The seat belts are bolted into position. Above the associate at the top right of the picture you can see the components for the MINI's curtain airbag system.

→ An assistor tool is used to position the dashboard within the cockpit.

Each kit of parts is unique and reflects the specification chosen by the customer.

Selecting parts

With thousands of components going into every MINI, each with their own unique part number, a system was needed that would not only help associates pick exactly the right combination of parts for each car on the assembly line but

→ The monitor above the assembly line indicates the model that has arrived at that particular assembly station and the parts that need to be selected.

→ The relevant parts are identified by graphics on the racking that correspond to those displayed on the monitor above the line.

would do so in a way that reduced worker fatigue and the chance of mistakes being made. The system chosen is a brilliantly simple one that assigns an easily recognised picture to each container of parts – anything from a rainbow to an ice-cream cone. A screen at each station not only signifies the model being assembled but also displays the pictures in the correct sequence required, meaning an associate can pick the parts quickly and accurately without having to scrutinise lengthy part numbers. When you consider that parts for the different models can look very similar, it's easy to see how such a system helps.

On a similar note, a system is also employed to highlight the fitting of infrequently used components – for example, one that's specific to a foreign market car – that could otherwise easily be missed. Once again, the line-side screen shows a visual reminder of the part, but an audible signal (perhaps a suitable tune) is also played through a speaker to alert the associate.

Assembly line tools

Fitting such a wide range of smaller components means various tools are required, from simple hand-held battery-powered items to more complex ones connected by cable to an external power supply. The tool chosen depends on the nature of the operation; for those that are safety-critical the tool will send information – usually via Wi-Fi – to a central database to confirm that the fixing was done up and to the correct torque (these are known as digitally controlled

tools). Any problems can be instantly identified and remedied before the vehicle travels any further along the assembly line. Tools are also specifically programmed for each task, and for each particular MINI model, so that they can't be used incorrectly or on the wrong model.

↑ The MINI's rear axle is assembled and tested in a separate area...

↓ ...before being raised into position and secured.

Stage 6

Having been moved by an exit lifter to a lower level, the cars are now transferred from the wooden skillet used so far to the ergonomic rotating sling for the first of the major mechanical parts to be fitted. We've arrived at what's known as Line 2, the rear suspension line, where the complete rear axle, suspension and brake assemblies will be married to the body. The rear axle carrier is assembled here, being fitted with parts such as brake lines, road springs, bump stops and anti-roll bar. Once complete, an assistor tool lifts the sub-assembled rear control arms (from Line 7) into position to be attached to the axle carrier, a task undertaken by associates and robotics using digitally controlled (DC) tools, bolting all of the various suspension arms into place. Maintaining the system of 'no

→ With the car mounted in the 'C-sling', operations such as fitting the brake and fuel pipes…

↓ …and the fuel tank, are made much easier.

fault forward', a number of camera stations ensure that the components and assembly are correct, an important part of the process as the next stage is the rear 'stuff-up' cell, where the rear axle will be attached to the body.

The 'coupling station' comes first, where the rear dampers are attached to the body via the top mountings, and then it's on to the 'securing station', where four robots bolt the rear axle carrier to the body. The final step is the 'decoupling station', where two associates have just 32 seconds to bolt the dampers to the rear suspension trailing arms. Once complete, the 'platten' that was supporting the axle carrier is lowered away and the body continues to the next stage robot station. Here, the rear suspension camber is checked and adjusted; the robot loosens the appropriate bolts, makes any adjustments and then re-tightens the bolts to the required torque.

With the slings mounted on an overhead conveyor, the cars are now rotated so that associates can begin fitting the numerous underbody parts, including brake and fuel lines, the fuel tank and some parts of the exhaust system. And because the cars are in the rotating sling associates can work on the roof at the same time, fitting parts such as the radio aerial. Like many of the processes in Final Assembly, all of these tasks are done by hand.

← The dashboard and centre console have been fitted, and work continues on fitting the remainder of the interior trim.

Stage 7

At Line 40 (or Skillet Line 2), the cars are transferred from the rotary slings back on to the wooden skillets as they continue their journey through assembly. At the stations that make up this line, and with the skillet-mounted flexi-lifts automatically adjusting in height for each operation, associates will be fitting a large number of parts including:

- The centre console.
- Interior trim panels, such as those covering the door pillars and sills.
- Interior switches and controls.

- The air-conditioning pipework from the engine bay to the cabin.
- Under-bonnet heat shields.
- Seat belts.
- Screen washer systems and front wiper motor.

The MINI will also get its headlining fitted, a part that has been supplied in sequence and that can only be fitted one way. A three-person operation, it's slid in through the windscreen aperture, secured in position and any wiring connections made. At this point items such as roof console switches and sun visor grab

↙ Here, associates are fitting the trim panels in the boot area of a five-door MINI.

↓ While interior trim is being fitted, other associates work to install the pipework for the car's cooling and air-conditioning systems.

← The headlining is lifted into position. This one is for a MINI equipped with a sunroof, but the operation is similar for all models.

handles are fitted. Two other key operations that take place at this stage are setting of the handbrake mechanism – a unique tool is fitted to the rear brakes to carry out the task – and electrical testing of the components installed so far, now being the ideal time to ensure that everything is working before the wiring and connectors get covered by further pieces of trim.

Stage 8

The car now arrives at the glass-fitting station, this time a robotised operation that takes place with the car stationary on the line. After the body flanges have been wiped with spirit to remove dirt and contaminants a robot measures the front and rear screen apertures so that the

← First operation at the glass-fitting station is the installation of the windscreen.

↙ The rear screen is fitted. Note the tape applied to the windscreen which prevents any movement while the bonding agent cures.

↓ Other glazing, such as the side glass seen here being fitted to a three-door MINI, is installed by hand.

correct screens are fitted according to model; there are also a number of windscreen types, some fitted with a rain sensor for example, so a dot code on each one is compared to the build specification. The next robot picks up the screen, placing it in front of a measuring device that then withdraws to be replaced by a gun that applies the bonding agent, which has been heated to 60°C. The front and rear screens are then fitted into place, and two pieces of pre-cut tape are automatically applied to hold the screens in place while the bonding cures. After fitting of the rear quarter glass on three-door models, the car continues to the next station for the addition of more trim parts. Once completed, it's back to the upper level where the cars are transferred from the wooden skillet to a sling in readiness for an important part of the assembly process.

Engine line and checking cell

With the engines having arrived from either Hams Hall (petrol versions), Steyr in Austria or Munich (diesels), they head for the engine line. Throughout this chapter of the manual there is mention of how sub-assemblies are used in the construction of a MINI – for example, in Body in White and Final Assembly – and it plays a major part in the engine lines, where more than 50 people are responsible for bringing together the engine, front suspension and brakes, front subframe and rear axle, which are then checked – both by camera and by hand – before heading to the main assembly line to be married to the appropriate body.

Rather than one sequential process of assembly, with parts being added at each successive station, this element of the production line sees a number of operations taking place in parallel. The main processes are as follows, although it's worth noting that some of them actually take place in other areas of assembly:

■ **Line 2** – here the rear axle carrier is assembled before being married to the body as explained in Stage 6.
■ **Low Level Line 3** – with the engines sequenced into the car assembly process, this is the first line where parts begin to be added, including attachment to the gearbox.
■ **Line 10** – although this appears to be out

of sequential line order, it's at this stage that gearboxes are fitted with a number of components, including clutch parts for manual transmissions.
■ **LAM Level Line 3** – transferred from the 'platten' on which they arrived to a hanging chain system for ease of access (height adjustable to aid ergonomics), it's here where a large number of components are fitted to the engine. These include items such as the alternator, starter motor, air-conditioning compressor, drive belts and pulleys, driveshafts, and emissions equipment

⬇ **Once the engines arrive from Hams Hall, they head to the separate Plant Oxford engine line.**

↑ **At LAM Level Line 3, numerous additional components and ancillaries will be fitted to each engine.**

↗ **Line 4 is where the front hub assemblies are constructed; this operation is sequenced to the build-up of the front axle carrier taking place on another line.**

↓ **At Line 5, the front axle carrier is fitted with a number of components including the steering rack as shown here…**

↘ **…and parts such as heat shields, all of which are fitted by hand.**

such as the catalytic convertor and diesel particulate filter as appropriate.

■ **Line 4** – a sub-assembly line, it's here where the front hubs are built up with the wheel bearings and brake assemblies. This is carried out in the same sequence as the engine and front suspension, as the complete hubs will meet those on the next line.

■ **Line 5** – arriving here via the engine transfer station, further engine dressing takes place and a number of pipework and electrical connections are made, including those for the cooling system. The coolant module containing the radiator and air-conditioning condenser will be fitted here, and the gearbox will be filled with a predetermined

quantity of lubricant. This is a very complex and busy line, as it's also where the front axle carrier is fitted with numerous parts, including the suspension lower control arms, the steering rack, the anti-roll bar and a number of heat shields. An assistor tool is then used to locate the hub assembly on to the driveshafts and axle carrier. Line 5 is also the location of a transfer cell where the now mostly complete engine and gearbox are joined to the front subframe/axle carrier, the whole unit mounted on a 'C-sling' as it travels towards its rendezvous with the body.

■ **Line 6** – this is where front suspension sub-assembly takes place, with the main processes as follows:

♦ The front strut body is mounted into a carrier and a guide pin is fitted.
♦ The spring is slotted over the damper rod.
♦ A protective rubber gaiter is fitted over the damper rod.
♦ The top mount is fitted.
♦ The strut moves forward to a camera cell for validation of parts and assembly.
♦ A tool compresses the spring for an associate to remove the guide pin and secure the main top nut.

■ **Line 7** – part of the rear axle assembly process, it's on this line that the sub-assembly of the wheel hubs, wheel bearings, brake discs and calipers and lower suspension control arms come together.

↖ **The front damper assembly process. The gaiter being fitted will prevent dirt ingress and premature wear to the damper rod and seals.**

↑ **An associate fits the top damper mounting. Assembly of front struts takes place in pairs for a specific vehicle, and they will soon be ready to be built into the front suspension.**

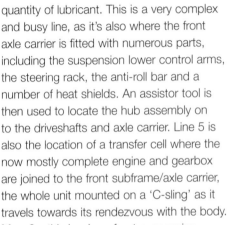

← **The parts for front strut assembly are stored as complete kits, helping to make construction quicker and easier for the associate.**

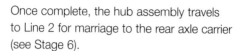

→ Some of the models built at Plant Oxford are equipped with the ALL4 four-wheel-drive system. Here, a propeller shaft awaits fitting.

Once complete, the hub assembly travels to Line 2 for marriage to the rear axle carrier (see Stage 6).

■ **Line 8** – A low-level line where the front axle for the four-wheel-drive ALL4 model is assembled, including the fitting of the propshaft.

It's worth noting here that the engine line actually 'over-produces' the powertrain assemblies; that is, it operates slightly quicker than the main assembly line – the cycle time for each operation is 64 seconds, a few seconds faster than main assembly – enabling the engine line to build up a 'buffer' of completed sub-assemblies. A mixture of automated and manual processes is used, the latter carried out by associates using digitally controlled (DC) tools that not only ensure the correct torque is used for each fixing but each operation can be monitored as part of the plant's 'no fault forward' system.

The completed modules then head to a separate cell where each one is checked by two robots. Using high-definition cameras, around 20 different points can be checked and compared with reference pictures to ensure that components are correctly fitted and aligned, the latter crucial as problems here would affect installation into the vehicle. A final 'quality gate' sees an associate undertake a visual examination of the entire assembly. Any rectification required is carried out at this point,

↑ To ensure that the components have been correctly fitted, every engine assembly is checked by high-definition robotic cameras...

→ ...and by hand. A final inspection of the complete engine assembly build. Any faults will be rectified here before the engine progresses further to meet the body.

with a record of any faults discovered fed into the monitoring system for further evaluation.

Stage 9

The car is now at an important stage of becoming a finished MINI, as it arrives at the section known as 'front marriage'. With pictures from the checking cell having confirmed the correct location of the engine and suspension on the subframe, the 'platten' (or 'mechanical module support') on which it's mounted is locked into place and the subframe and engine are lifted into position from below. Accuracy is vital to achieve perfect alignment of the powertrain and body, so the first operation is pre-alignment, which sees the assembly raised to 6in below the body, with a robot checking the alignment; this is the coupling station. An associate is also on hand to monitor the process and can intervene if any issues are spotted.

The MINI now moves forward into the securing station where it meets four robots automatically loaded with the eight securing bolts, the subframe is fixed into position, and the very heart of a MINI is in place. However, the whole assembly will remain attached to the carrying platten while the car moves forward again into the decoupling station, where an associate has secured the front suspension top mounts to the body. At this point cars equipped with the ALL4 four-wheel-drive system will have the propeller shaft fitted, a component that incorporates a short telescopic section to enable easy fitting. Then the complete exhaust

↓ **The engine and body arrive at 'front marriage' during the carefully sequenced assembly process. Accurate alignment is vital before the unit is secured in place.**

→ The next stages of assembly see the cars mounted in specially designed 'Z-frames', allowing easy access to the relevant areas of the vehicle.

→→ Components fitted at this stage include the heavy battery which is swung into position using an assistor tool.

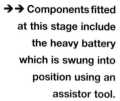

→ A similar assistor tool is also used to locate the front-end module prior to securing into place.

system is fitted and the system checked for rattles and incorrect alignment. It's also at this point that the engine starts to become joined to the body via the numerous pipes and electrical connections that go into every car.

Stage 10

With the cars now attached to a 'Z-frame' – here it's the frames that move the cars along and not the floor – the MINI is about to receive plenty more parts as it inches closer to completion. First come items such as the battery, and then the car is ready for the front-end module incorporating the bumper and grille; assembled at a separate factory in Banbury, the module also includes components such as the cooling fan, the bonnet release cable and latch and the driving lights located in the front bumper. Lifted into position by an associate using an assistor frame, it's bolted into place using a hand-held electric tool.

It's also worth mentioning that this front-end module is a true demonstration of the 'just-in-time' build process. With a lead time of less than two hours before the module is required on the assembly line – which includes transport from Banbury – the time allowed for actual production is exceptionally tight. Minimal stock is held at Plant Oxford, enough for approximately 20 minutes' worth of production, and the parts arrive in the correct sequence for Final Assembly. They are delivered to the assembly line by a tow train carrying 12 modules at a time.

Stage 11

Now at Line 50, the seats have arrived from Birmingham, once again in exactly the right sequence for the car being assembled. First to be fitted are the rear bench and squab, and then the front seats are swung into position using an assistor tool and bolted into place by the associate, using a hand-held electric tool. At this stage the wiring connection beneath

↑ Tow trains deliver completed front end modules to the assembly line. This is an impressive demonstration of the 'just in time' assembly process employed at Plant Oxford.

← At Line 50 the seats are fitted. Rears are mounted first, followed by the fronts.

↑ Once any electrical connections have been made, the rear bumper is located and fixed into position by hand.

the seat – for the air bag system and items like seat heating – will have been connected, and at the next station an associate will fit items such as the fuel-filler neck, screen wash bottles and the wheel-arch liners. The toolkit, first aid kit and owner's information pack are also added.

Next comes the rear bumper, once again a component that arrives on the assembly line in the correct build sequence. But unlike the larger, heavier front end module this will be fitted by hand by two associates, who locate it on to pre-fitted brackets and screw it into place. And as with many of the stations on the assembly line, it's not just one process that takes place; as the bumper is being fitted other associates are securing sill trims and connecting the steering column to the steering rack.

↓ The box visible on the dashboard downloads software via the car's on-board diagnostics socket.

Stage 12

Transferred to an upper level, the cars now travel the length of the assembly building where they are about to join Line 51, the penultimate line in the process that has taken a bare bodyshell and turned it into a complete, functioning MINI. But as you might expect, there is still plenty to do before the car is finished:

■ The securing bolts for the front seats are tightened to their correct torque.
■ The tail-light units and steering wheel are fitted.
■ The alignment of the bonnet is checked and any minor adjustments made to ensure secure latching.
■ A small computer programming unit is plugged into the car's diagnostic socket, downloading relevant software as the car progresses down the line.
■ The driver's airbag unit is connected and secured into place.

Meanwhile a separate area is assembling the rearmost doors for the Clubman models, fitting them with items such as locks, latches and electrical components. Once complete, a powered assistor is used by an associate to manoeuvre the doors into position, and they are then bolted to the hinges. Just one door is fitted at a time here.

Stage 13

The car has now arrived at Line 52, where it's still being carried in the Z-cradle, and work begins on some small but important tasks such as fitting the final undertrays and the underbody panels that will protect the brake and fuel lines. Most importantly, though, this is where the wheels are fitted. Arriving in sequence as a complete set – an important point, as there's in the region of 42 different combinations of wheel in terms of size and design – they are loaded automatically on to an assistor, which the associate uses to position the wheels on the hub. He then swings an electrically operated 'multi-nut runner' tool into position, which once engaged with the wheel bolts will tighten all five at a time to exactly the right torque.

Now, on its own wheels for the very first time

since entering Final Assembly, the car can be released from the Z-cradle and transferred on to a moving conveyor where it's about to undergo another raft of important processes:

- The first station fills the car with vital fluids. Air-conditioning refrigerant, engine coolant and brake fluid are all added here, dispensed in pre-measured quantities depending on the model being assembled. The engine and gearbox have already been filled with oil on the engine line.
- A brake pressure test is performed using a dedicated meter that ensures brake pressure matches the force applied to the brake pedal; the results are recorded by an ICON box, which transmits the results to the monitoring database.
- The interior rear-view mirror and wiper arms are fitted.
- The headlights are fitted, loosely at first as they need to be correctly aligned with the apertures in the bonnet – whereas the first generation of MINI used headlights that were attached to the bonnet itself, and lifted with it, the current models have the lights mounted on the body with precisely positioned holes in the bonnet to fit over them. First the bonnet is closed and a securing jig fitted to each light; then a tool is attached to the jig and positions the light in exactly the right place for a perfect fit. The associate can then tighten the light retaining screws.
- Remember the doors that were removed way back at the beginning of the process and sent off to be assembled? Well, here is where they are reunited with the car, arriving on the line at exactly the right time to meet the car they were removed from – a perfect example of the amazingly detailed planning and timing that goes into the building of a MINI. The associate uses a powered assistor to lift each door from its rack (they are working on one side of the car only, with another associate fitting the doors on the other side), and after protective strips are applied to the edges to prevent paint damage they are swung into position and secured to the hinges with bolts, using an electric tool. In order to make best use of the 67-second cycle time, if the associate is

working on a three-door model he will carry out other tasks once the doors are fitted; if it's a five-door model he will fit both front and rear doors instead. The work at this station is completed by the fitting of any remaining external trim, for example the chrome strips below the side windows.

- The alignment of the door glass is checked by a dedicated jig; a lineside screen indicates any adjustment required by the associate.
- Each MINI is filled with a small amount of fuel (approximately 10–14 litres), just enough for it to complete any driving tasks. Interestingly, a UK car gets less fuel than one destined for, say, the US or Chinese markets, as those cars would usually need to be driven further during the delivery process.
- Next it's time for a series of electrical tests that will check, remotely via a pre-programmed test unit – the ICON box resting on the dashboard – the functions of items such as the electrically assisted power steering, the electric windows and the engine sensors. Some programming of electronic control units (ECUs) will also be taking place. This is the first time that the engine will be run in the car, so for this stage an extractor unit is lowered from the ceiling to safely channel exhaust gases away from the assembly area.

With these tasks completed successfully, the completed MINI is driven from the line and heads for final testing and validation. The long and complex journey all the way from Body in White is almost over.

↑ This MINI will soon be rolling on its wheels for the first time. The wheels are fitted using a specially designed tool that locates and tightens all the wheel bolts.

↖ We are almost at the end of the assembly process, and here the car is being filled with vital fluids.

↑ While fluid filling takes place, associates fit the headlamps.

← Remember those doors we saw being assembled earlier? Here they are being reunited with the correct car; an assistor tool makes light work of manoeuvring these weighty components.

↓ Each MINI is filled with just enough fuel for testing and delivery purposes.

↓ An associate proudly adds the finishing touch. Assembly has been a complex process and there are just a few final stages remaining.

→ Final testing and programming includes checks of the electrically assisted power steering; the system will be a run through a pre-programmed series of tests.

↓ The finished car is driven from the end of the assembly line. This is just one of the 1,000 MINIs that leave Plant Oxford every day.

↓↓ After leaving the assembly line, each car heads to final testing and validation before it is ready to be sent to the customer.

Cockpit assembly

Known within Plant Oxford as the cockpit, it's better known to drivers as the fascia or dashboard. As already mentioned, it's lifted into the vehicle using an assistor tool before being bolted into place, and arrives at the assembly line on a computer-controlled automated guided vehicle (AGV). But it's a component that is also assembled – by hand, and directly on to an AGV – within the plant.

When an empty AGV arrives at cockpit assembly the first step is to mount the aluminium crossbeam and frame to which all other components are attached. First to be added is the wiring harness for the switches and instruments (this will be connected to the main harness on the assembly line), followed by the steering column. Next to be added is the heating, ventilation and air-conditioning unit (HVAC), which is bolted to the crossbeam. Then the dash-top moulding is fitted. With all of the main parts in place it's then a case of fitting the raft of components that make up the finished assembly, including the instrument cluster, the centre console and bracketry for the infotainment system, the column stalks, the glovebox and the passenger airbag unit. This having taken around nine minutes to complete, the AGV heads back to the assembly line with a finished cockpit ready for installation.

Seat assembly

Unless they are particularly uncomfortable the seats in a car rarely get much consideration, but for the purposes of this manual they are yet another part of the logistical challenge involved in building a MINI. Manufactured by a supplier in Banbury, Oxfordshire, and delivered to Plant Oxford on a just-in-time basis, the number of variations is mind-boggling. There are manual and electrically adjustable versions, heated or non-heated, and assorted different styles, such as the sporting type used in John Cooper Works models, and that's before you even start to consider the vast range of colour and material choices. Oh, and don't forget that building cars for global markets means there are various different safety regulations to consider too.

Five days from production, the supplier receives the orders for customer cars and the build process gets under way. A logistics system picks the correct components and materials for the seats being made, with all of the parts scanned to ensure that they are not only correct but conform to regulations in the car's final destination. One hundred and twenty sets (a pair of front seats, along with the rear seat base and backrest) will then be built in a continuous process. Sub-assembly lines undertake a number of tasks such as preparing the seat frame, fitting the covers to the seat foam and adding items such as airbag units, heating elements and height-adjustment controls.

The front seats then head to the main assembly lines, where the build continues with all of the necessary fastenings and trim sections added while further lines construct the matching rear seats. Once complete it heads to testing, where the electrical and adjustment functions are checked and any required programming is carried out (for example, cars destined for the US have a weight detector that controls airbag

↓ **Construction of the dashboard takes place on an automated guided vehicle (AGV)…**

↓↓ **…which will then deliver the finished unit to the assembly line ready for fitting.**

deployment depending on whether a child or adult is in the seat). The set for each vehicle is then loaded on to a pallet that will head to a buffer area before awaiting the journey to Plant Oxford. Each truck carries 60 such pallets which are loaded in a reverse sequence, so that when they are unloaded they are in the correct sequence for assembly. Around 16 trucks head to Oxford every day, leaving at hourly intervals.

The Final Assembly control room

Overseeing the Final Assembly of 1,000 cars every day is no easy task, which is why this area of the plant has its own control room. Located adjacent to the end of the main assembly line – so as centrally as possible to operations – it is manned by two people and undertakes a number of tasks. The first is to monitor the feeds from a raft of CCTV cameras positioned at various stations along the assembly line, at points where it would be inefficient to have associates constantly monitoring the work taking place. Should a control room operator spot a problem or stoppage on one of the cameras they can deploy a member of the maintenance team to deal with it.

The other key task within the control room is to monitor and assess the messages fed back by all of the major tooling used on the assembly line. Apart from the small hand tools, all of the other equipment – such as the larger digitally controlled tools, the assistors and the slings – collates information on their operation and, via the process logic control system that manages all of the equipment, feeds back details to the control room. The tools constantly self-check for any processes or operations not undertaken as expected – things that could be caused by a fault with the tool, an associate not completing a task or a car not moving on the line. If a problem is detected an error message is sent to the control room, although the tools will also send a constant stream of messages confirming that everything is okay.

At the same time, sensors located on other pieces of machinery monitor parameters such as temperature during operation, allowing control room operators to spot potential problems before they become serious. With so much equipment being used, this adds up to millions of messages being sent every day, so they are prioritised and

colour-coded for display on the large screen in the control room, allowing operators to quickly identify issues. The operators also record and monitor any production stoppages, allowing them to assess whether production efficiency targets are being met (expressed as a gross potential number, effectively the total production hours per day multiplied by the number of cars made per hour).

Being able to monitor issues that could affect production targets allows operators to identify problem areas and helps in prioritising maintenance repairs, minimising any downtime. The control system is so clever that it is even able to send text messages to managers' phones on an hourly basis, updating them on performance.

Testing and validation

With all of the work on the assembly line complete, all that's left at this stage is for each MINI to undergo a final series of checks and adjustments before it heads to final validation and road testing.

The process begins with associates from Body in White checking every inch of the panels, with a particular focus on the alignment and fit of the doors, bonnet and tailgate. Panel gaps and shut-lines are measured with gauges to identify any areas considered sub-standard, the associates being able to make small adjustments to hinges if necessary. Clearly, large discrepancies would be a sign of problems much earlier in the build process, and would need detailed investigation. However, such issues would be very rare at this stage of the build given the quality control mechanisms employed at each stage, so the checks here are about ensuring maximum quality before a car heads to the customer.

Every car then heads to the test suite,

↑ Inside the control room at Final Assembly, where a breath-taking amount of information is received and monitored.

→ At testing and validation, panel and component gaps are checked for accuracy.

↑ Both wheel and headlamp alignment are undertaken at the same station.

↓ In a rolling-road chamber, an associate checks various operations, following a test program displayed on a screen.

↘ Another rolling road checks braking functions.

where the first operation takes place on the laser alignment rig. Here, the settings for wheel alignment (or tracking), toe and camber angles are checked using sophisticated equipment, while an associate positioned in a pit beneath the car makes the necessary adjustments to ensure alignment is spot-on.

While this is taking place, another associate checks and adjusts the headlamp beam settings. Then the car heads for a sealed chamber containing a rolling road where, after the identification label has been scanned to confirm the model being tested, a driver will follow a pre-set test program displayed on a screen (much like the process undertaken when tests are carried out to establish official fuel economy figures). The tests take only a couple of minutes. Some of them might be market-specific, depending on the country for which the car is destined, but all involve the driver cycling through a number of parameters from acceleration and braking to engagement of each of the gears. The tests take the vehicle up to a speed of around 90mph. Then the car heads to another rolling road for braking and ABS function tests, and once that's complete the last check is on the audio and in-car entertainment functions.

Job rotation

The age of workers on car assembly lines spending many hours a day completing repetitive tasks may be over – in part thanks to the automation of many processes – but job rotation still plays an important role at Plant Oxford. Assembly is a skilled process where quality is paramount, so training associates in a number of different roles brings numerous benefits, including a reduction in physical and mental stress; improved versatility, so that an associate can step into a specific role at short notice; and the ability to assist other associates should they experience a problem. Learning a range of tasks is also useful for anyone considering career progression, for example becoming a Lead Associate.

Lead Associates

Having experienced associates on the assembly line (there is one for every dozen or so workers) who can step in whenever a problem occurs is an important part of keeping the line moving efficiently. But there are also other key aspects to their role. With each assembly station having at least one Lead Associate, they act as a first point of contact between workers and management and can help solve a variety of issues, such as someone struggling to undertake a task because of, say, a fault with tooling. They can also pass ideas up the management chain if someone identifies a more efficient way of doing things, something that all associates are encouraged to do. With safety being so important in such a busy environment, Lead Associates also take responsibility for ensuring there are no hazards that could endanger workers, and assisting should an accident occur.

In addition the Lead Associate can undertake any task within their area should another worker be unavailable, and play an important role in maintaining the quality of the cars as they travel through Final Assembly. For example, they ensure that associates are correctly dressed, with no exposed belt-buckles or watches that could cause damage, even ensuring that visitors to the line adhere to these same rules. Being a Lead Associate is an important role, then, one that helps ensure the process of assembling a MINI is as smooth as possible, with attention to quality always uppermost.

Andon system

With such complex tasks being undertaken in a limited time it's perhaps inevitable that minor problems can occur, anything from an incorrect component being supplied to a machine tool breaking down. Resolving such issues as quickly as possible is key, which is why the

AMY DRUCE

PROCESS LEADER

Not only was Amy the first female Lead Associate in Final Assembly, she was the first Process Leader there too, and she has worked at Plant Oxford for rather longer than she first imagined: 'Although I'd had family working at the plant I wasn't really sure what I wanted to do and only joined in a temporary role. It was only supposed to last for three months, and my friends actually had a sweepstake on how long I'd last, but I soon realised that I was enjoying the job, and have now been here for 14 years. I'd quickly realised that the work was physical but it's all about your attitude to it, and to be honest the structured approach of the tasks actually suits me. But the other great thing is the camaraderie you have with colleagues. It's a really sociable environment where you feel part of a family, and you also know that everyone is working together to produce the best possible product. That's a good feeling, and it's also been nice to progress through different roles with the same people I knew at the very beginning. I still really enjoy the role, and can't see myself leaving, and in any case there are still plenty of other areas within assembly that I want to work in.'

assembly line at Plant Oxford uses an 'Andon' system. A Japanese word that translates as 'sign' or 'signal' in English, it was part of Toyota's pioneering quality control system and essentially consists of a cable (reminiscent of the bell on a Routemaster bus, for those old enough to remember such things!) or buttons located along the assembly line, which workers can activate if they experience a problem at their particular station. The resultant visual signal alerts the Lead Associate, who responds and resolves the problem.

← This cable, fitted alongside the assembly line, is part of the Andon system.

ANDREW ROBINSON

TOLERANCE MANAGEMENT ENGINEER

A scientist by trade, Andrew's role at Plant Oxford is a key one when it comes to the quality of every MINI: 'I'm a physics graduate and before this worked at the National Physical Laboratory, where I focused on metrology, working closely with both automotive and aerospace fields. Back in 2013 I was approached by BMW about a role here and felt the time was right to move across to the car industry and I had something to contribute. Today my focus is on the theoretical side of dimensional metrology and vehicle tolerances and it's something I find satisfying and very stimulating. And it's certainly a big cultural change from the NPL – there I had more time to explore theories, whereas here it's much more about tight deadlines, with more pressure on solving problems quickly. I thrive on it, and enjoy seeing the impact of my work on the finished product.'

→ **Hand-held tools can be used to examine the fit and alignment of components.**

↓ **Laser scanners can focus on a very specific aspect of a MINI's bodyshell, as here.**

METROLOGY

Just what is metrology, and what part does it play in the building of a MINI? Well, its definition is the 'science of measurement', and it provides engineers within the quality department at Plant Oxford with a number of analysis tools that provide a method of verifying the quality of the product, ensuring that every single car is consistent to within agreed tolerances when it comes to shape, size and dimensional accuracy. It enables the constant scrutiny of things like panel gaps and the fit of components, and ensures that every MINI meets the specifications laid down by both designers and the processes designed at the very outset of production.

An example of these specifications is the 'Fugenplan' (or 'Gap Plan') which, as the name implies, specifies the gaps between separate panels, body sections and components. Car makers go to great lengths to ensure these gaps are as tight and consistent as possible, as they play a key part in a customer's perception of vehicle quality. Therefore measurement analysts in the metrology department have a number of tools available that will help them assess and maintain that quality. These range from hand-held laser gauges and probes used on specific areas of bodywork or the interior (some tools are specifically designed to assist in optical checks, where flexible parts such as seals, headlining or carpets would be impossible to measure with contact probes) to robot-mounted probes and laser scanners to examine larger areas of a vehicle.

Portable probes/scanners mounted on articulated arms also allow measurements to be taken on the assembly line itself, making it easier to work within the limitations imposed by the 67-second process time (or 'takt time' as it's referred to within the plant, although there are a number of measurements that can be taken during this time). However, pre-planned checks can also be undertaken outside of production hours – for example, the portable tools could be used to check the reproducibility of the windscreen installation (*ie* that each installation is exactly the same) by monitoring the process during multiple fittings.

Perhaps one of the most impressive tools is the optical scanning process. Here, a car (preferably one that's painted white, as it prevents unwanted reflections confusing the scanner) is mounted on a turntable and then covered with a number of dots and crosses that make up a reference framework. The entire surface of the car is then examined by a robot-mounted scanner in a series of separate sections, which are then stitched together to form one complete three-dimensional image of the body. By representing the measurements as a colour map of the car body – for example, areas within tolerance are shown in green and potential deviations from original specifications highlighted in red or blue – engineers can quickly identify any issues and begin the process of investigating where in the manufacturing or assembly processes the problems are being caused.

↑ Those same laser scanners can also be employed to assess the dimensional accuracy of complete bodies.

↓ Here, the optical scanning process is taking place; the result is an incredibly accurate 3D image.

Costing in the region of £1 million and weighing almost 3.5 tonnes depending on model, the Pruefcube is a full-size MINI body made entirely from aluminium and machined to within 0.2mm of accuracy to the original design specification.

Its role within the metrology department is twofold. Firstly it's employed during the development phase of a new model when components are fitted to it to understand exactly how they will fit together during assembly; at this stage it's a vital tool in assessing the quality of parts to decide whether changes need to be made, so it's expected that a new model will be assembled this way three or four times prior to full production so that any problems – either with the components themselves or with the way in which they are fitted together – can be eradicated before production begins.

Secondly, the Pruefcube plays an important role in ensuring quality is maintained throughout series production. Not only does it provide a consistently accurate reference point for engineers but it can also be used to iron out problems that might occur. For example, should an issue arise with the fitting of a specific component it can quickly be tried on the Pruefcube to establish whether the problem lies with the component itself, the car body or the fitting process. It's this ability to rapidly identify and correct problems that contributes to the Plant Oxford philosophy of 'right first time'.

↑ Made from aluminium, each Pruefcube can represent a whole or partial body.

← The Pruefcubes play a vital role in the quality of every MINI leaving Plant Oxford.

← An associate can use the Pruefcubes to test the fit of components before assembly processes are finalised.

↓ The accurate fitting of the interior components is as important as the exterior. Here, you can see the framework to which the dashboard is fitted.

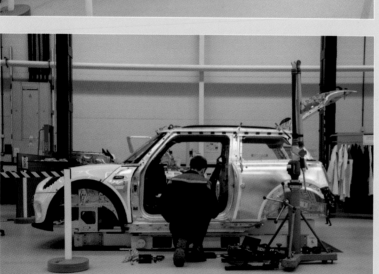

QUALITY CONTROL

Today's car buyers take quality and reliability for granted. They expect their cars to operate efficiently and without any problems in all weathers and conditions, and provide years of reliable service without suffering the sort of annoying failures that dogged cars in the past. And as cars have become more complex, efficient, comfortable and stuffed with every conceivable luxury and convenience feature, it has become ever harder to meet buyers' expectations. In fact, it's not so many years ago that vehicles suffered from distinctly sub-standard cabin refinement, making long journeys pretty wearing ordeals, not to mention the sort of creaks and rattles from flimsy plastic trim that would be anathema to today's owners. Indeed, take a trip in a model built at Cowley in the 1970s or 1980s (and plenty of other car factories of the time, if we're being fair) and it is easy to see just how much things have changed.

Thankfully, Plant Oxford is a very different place where an amazing amount of time and effort is devoted to ensuring that not only is a MINI fun to drive but that it will remain that way for many years. Millions of miles of testing are carried out around the world before a new model is launched, but there is also plenty of work that can be done at the factory. Some of this takes place in the Quality and Engineering Centre, in a process that MINI refer to as 'Total Vehicle Quality'. Let's take a closer look at just what this involves.

Road simulator

Known within quality control as the 'shaker rig', this piece of equipment is used to test both development models and production cars. With a car mounted on the rig, each corner is subjected to a pummelling that replicates the vehicle driving on rough roads, which is the ideal way of checking for squeaks and rattles from interior trim and fittings. The rig is computer-controlled and runs through a predetermined test sequence, usually with one or two people inside the vehicle using sensitive electronic microphones to check for any noises. By enabling testing to be done in a controlled environment it both eliminates the problem of

↑ A high-performance John Cooper Works model being tested on the shaker rig.

external noises you'd get driving on the road and is somewhat safer than trying to identify the source of a rattle whilst driving!

Not only is the rig a useful tool for establishing quality prior to series production getting under way, it is also used when new or updated parts are fitted. During the regular Model Year updates that most cars receive the team can ensure that changes to trim and equipment won't have any adverse effects on quality, for example by introducing rattles that didn't exist previously.

↓ Sensitive microphones pick up any noises from interior trim. Eliminating the potential for annoying squeaks and rattles is a vital part of the quality-control process.

↑ **A Cooper S inside the acoustic chamber. Both good and bad noises can be analysed here.**

Acoustic dynamometer

Costing in the region of £3 million to install – the single biggest investment in quality control facilities at Plant Oxford – this clever piece of equipment allows the car to be 'driven' without anyone actually being inside. The dyno can run at up to 160mph and is located within a chamber that's constructed from 215mm thick concrete walls, with a further 450mm of fibreglass sound proofing. And the purpose of all this expensive technology? Well, it's all about the acoustic performance of a MINI,

and by placing microphones around the car's interior the team can simulate a customer being inside and get an objective measurement of the sounds that are created.

Rating the sounds on a scale of one to ten, not only can engineers identify the sorts of noises that would irritate a driver or passengers – excessive road or engine noise, for example – but they can also fine-tune the 'good' noises that can enhance the driving experience. With MINIs renowned for their sporting characteristics a degree of intake rasp when the driver extends the engine, or a pleasing burble from the exhaust when the 'sport' mode is selected, can all add to the enjoyment. This acoustic chamber is used both prior to full production getting under way and during production, to check that cars still conform to engineering specifications.

Water testing

There are few things more annoying for car owners than finding that water leaks into the cabin. Not only can this damage trim and cause condensation, but there's also the potential for it to play havoc with delicate electronic components. Which is why Plant Oxford has the facility to test cars in everything from a light drizzle to the heaviest of monsoon conditions.

Tests can range from spending six hours spraying the car with three litres of water a minute – equivalent to a light shower – to ten minutes at up to 50 litres a minute, replicating the most extreme conditions a car is likely to experience. (The water used for the test is captured and recycled for future use.) Used

↓ **Water testing can replicate everything from the lightest shower…**

↘ **…to full-on monsoon conditions, with not a drop being allowed to enter the cabin.**

← Testing can involve some very chilly temperatures. A modern MINI must be able to function in all conditions without a problem.

during both the development phase for new models and to test samples of production cars, the water testing chamber can carry out a number of tests with the vehicle in different positions – since each body design has its own characteristics it's important to check that water hitting the vehicle from a particular angle doesn't lead to ingress into the cabin, or that water running off panels doesn't collect in the wrong places. With an associate inside the car examining door and window seals with an endoscope (a camera mounted on a flexible probe) as the test takes place, the team can ensure that no water is getting in. And just in case the worst happens and the car should start filling with water, the associate will use the car's horn to attract attention!

Temperature testing

Before a new car makes it into production it's almost certain that the development teams will have spent many months checking its operation in some of the harshest climates in the world. At Plant Oxford some of that work can be replicated in the climate chamber, where MINIs can be subjected to a very chilly –40°C up to a scorching 90°C. Not that such extreme temperatures are used very often, as there is the safety of the engineers to consider, but being able to test a vehicle's functions in such extreme conditions ensures that future owners are very unlikely to experience problems. Nor is it only temperature that is tested, as the chamber can also vary the humidity, right up to a driver-drenching 95% relative humidity.

Using a pre-programmed test sequence, many of the tests are designed to check electrical functions, but they also focus on issues such as ice build-up, engine ignition, the operation of door handles and the opening of doors and windows. So the next time you complain about a British winter you can be confident that your MINI has already experienced the worst the weather can throw at it.

Road testing

The tests carried out so far are certainly rigorous, but to supplement them every car that leaves Final Assembly will also be subjected to a road test on a specially designed track located behind the Paint Shop. The test begins with a check of exterior and interior components – items such as mirrors, light units, wiper arms and switches – to check their security and, to a limited degree, their function. Once happy that everything has been fitted and works correctly, the associate will take the car through a predetermined test sequence.

Using a covered tunnel to reflect noise, the car is driven over a variety of different surfaces from rough paving to rumble strips and 'train tracks', each one designed to cause different levels of vibration and expose any rattles and squeaks from the trim and fittings. Should any problems be discovered the car heads for a rectification bay where associates can examine the vehicle and establish the cause of unwanted noises. If further analysis is required the team might also use the shaker rig described previously.

→ Just a few of the many trucks that arrive at Plant Oxford every day delivering parts from all over the world.

→ Unloading is a non-stop process.

⬇ Thousands of parts are unloaded on a daily basis. These components are heading for the warehouse and could be on the assembly line in a matter of hours.

LOGISTICS

I t's probably fair to say that anyone thinking about what goes into building a modern car isn't going to spend much time dwelling on the matter of logistics. It's hardly a glamorous subject, is it? But when you're running a factory that builds 1,000 vehicles a day it's an absolutely vital part of the process, and you don't have to spend long in the logistics department of Plant Oxford to realise what an overwhelmingly complex task it is.

Just think about it for a moment. This is a car factory that relies on the delivery of parts (some 500,000 will move through the warehouse every day) from more than 500 suppliers in 27 countries, all of which arrive at the plant in 270 lorries per day. And if that wasn't enough, MINI operate a 'just-in-time' system whereby parts are scheduled to arrive just a couple of hours before they will be needed to build a car. Developed by Japanese car maker Toyota, it's a system used by many factories across the world and is intended to make the production process as efficient as possible by reducing stock levels held on site. With Plant Oxford holding just two hours of production supply on some key components, it's a system that's not without significant risk.

So just how does the plant manage the challenges involved and ensure that production doesn't grind to a halt? Well, that job falls to

Facts and figures

- More than 500 suppliers provide the parts to build MINIs.
- Parts arrive from 27 countries.
- There are more than 14,000 active part numbers used in the assembly hall at Plant Oxford.
- Around 270 lorries per day deliver parts. They arrive in hourly time slots.
- 27,000 pallets of parts move through the assembly hall each week.
- On average 2,200 full containers and 13,000 small boxes of parts are delivered to the line every day.
- Around 170,000 parts are picked and sequenced to the assembly line every day.

↑ The skilled logistics team monitors hundreds of deliveries, and can react at a moment's notice to maintain the flow of parts. Any delays in production could prove very costly.

the logistics department, whose work begins with detailed forecasting of exactly what will be needed when, so that suppliers can provide parts accordingly. With the annual requirements decided, the forecast is fine-tuned at the monthly, weekly and daily level, and the 'just-in-time' suppliers are given a 'call-off' for the particular order six days before the daily batch of cars is due to be built; this is a detailed parts requirement that will enable production to go ahead with supplies timed to an hourly window, with some flexibility for the sequence of the parts delivery to be altered should the build slot for a particular car be changed.

The scheduling system is IT-based but with a manual back-up, and operates on a two-way system that sends parts demands to suppliers and allows those suppliers to confirm despatch (known in the business as the 'advance shipping notice'). With such tight timescales and little room for error, constant monitoring is required so that the logistics team can see exactly how much stock they have (the stock of 'just-in-time' parts is checked on a minute-by-minute basis, for example), and the system includes various 'triggers' that will alert them to potential problems and enable a solution to be found.

Take, for example, the delivery of completed front-end modules that are produced in a factory in Banbury located around 30 miles from Plant Oxford. A truck loaded with completed modules

STEVE PROSSER

MATERIAL SUPPLY MANAGER

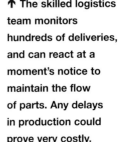

Steve has been in the supply and logistics business for over 25 years, but that isn't where it all started:

'I went into banking for about three years after leaving school and then decided to go to university where I got a business degree, and managed to enjoy a bit of time playing rugby there too! My father worked in purchasing and supply at the Oxford plant and I guess it's in my blood, so it's no surprise that I ended up in the car industry by joining a management scheme at the Rover factory at Longbridge (and continuing the theme my eldest son is now a Business Apprentice with BMW). In fact, we always had Rovers and other BL models as family cars, so it was a nice connection. When BMW took over the business I moved across to the Oxford plant, and already being used to their way of doing things the transition into logistics here was quite easy. I'd say I'm definitely a logistics man through and through!'

➜ Racks of carpets await their new homes in finished MINIs.

➜ Crates of components are in constant demand.

➜ While some parts head straight to the assembly line, others are stacked in the warehouse. They won't be here for long, though.

leaves the Banbury site every 37 minutes and their journey down the M40 motorway is closely monitored. Not only are the logistics team able to watch traffic conditions in real time thanks to access to the feeds from roadside cameras, but each lorry is tracked so that should a traffic hold-up occur the vehicle can be re-routed to ensure it arrives at Plant Oxford on time. And then there are the parts that arrive from the factories on the Continent, usually via the port of Calais. Again, the process is closely monitored, and along with alerts from freight companies the logistics team work closely with port authorities to understand potential problems and find solutions. These could take the form of diverting supplies to another port, or even an airport if necessary; whatever it takes to ensure that cars continue to roll down the production line. Making sure that happens is a simply huge undertaking, and a fascinating part of what goes into building a MINI.

So what happens to the parts once they arrive at Plant Oxford? Well, the way they are handled depends on the demands of the assembly process. Some parts that are required 'just-in-time' – seats, for example – will be automatically loaded straight on to a conveyor that will take them to the assembly line, while other less urgent components will enter a 'buffer' area. If parts are destined for the on-site warehouse they will either be stacked or put on special racks, the warehouse operating on what's known as a 'first-in first-out' (FIFO) system, with parts used in order of delivery, and parts are called to the line based on demand. That demand is triggered by the painted bodies arriving at the assembly line, the system calculating the parts that will be required and delivering them to the relevant fitting area as needed.

Parts in the warehouse are picked by hand or by forklift truck, depending on size, and are then loaded into delivery containers ready for despatch; an 'Andon board' (or signal board) will tell the delivery driver when they should leave the warehouse. Tow trains then deliver them to the appropriate area on the assembly line, each one pulling either full containers (five at a time for standard size, or three at a time for oversize containers) or a small number of trolleys carrying smaller boxes of parts; each trolley holds 36 boxes. Each train – following a specific route and delivery schedule – will deliver a mixture of parts to ensure that there is no over-stocking of particular components at the line.

↑ **More carpets arrive at Plant Oxford, the white undersides visible in this photograph.**

↑ **A system of tow trains is used to deliver components to Final Assembly.**

↓ **With such a large number of tow trains leaving the warehouse at any one time, a dedicated system is used to control departures.**

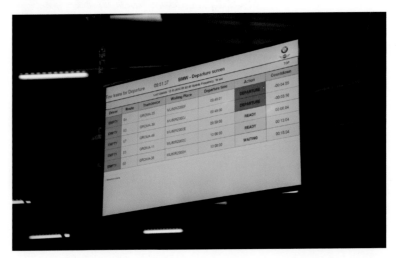

↑ Covered in protective film, finished MINIs await transport to customers in the UK and around the world.

CARS LEAVING PLANT OXFORD

So far in this section we've looked at all the parts that come into the factory, but what happens when it comes to finished vehicles leaving? Referred to as 'outbound logistics', there's a whole industry within Plant Oxford dedicated to getting the 1,000 cars built every day delivered to their new owners across the UK and the world. Since 2001, more than three million MINIs have been exported to 110 countries – around 80% of production – and it's no easy task.

So how is this achieved? Well, with the bodywork protected from damage during transit by the use of a protective film, the finished cars are transported to the plant's loading area, where they are sorted by destination and country.

→ Some cars leave Plant Oxford on conventional transporters...

From there 20 conventional transporter lorries – each carrying 11 vehicles – will deliver cars within the UK, with a further 18 transporters delivering cars to ports at Southampton Docks and Immingham near Grimsby. Fifteen ships per week leave the UK loaded with new MINIs, with the majority of the 800 cars exported each day leaving from Southampton. However, around 20 cars per day head from Immingham to Sweden and Denmark; up to 15 are sent from Portbury, Bristol, to Portugal; and from Immingham cars destined for Russia and Eastern Europe leave bound for Zeebrugge in Belgium. And that's not all, as around ten cars, loaded into containers, leave from the port of London Gateway bound for Brazil, and a smaller number depart from other ports around the UK for destinations such as the Bahamas. Some cars are even flown to customers!

Perhaps more exciting, though, is that 60% of the vehicles destined for export leave Plant Oxford via its very own train service. The two double-decker trains – each of them around 680m long – that leave the plant every day (there's a train to Southampton every morning from Monday to Saturday, and one to Purfleet every afternoon between Monday and Friday)

each carry around 290 very carefully loaded cars. Joining the main national rail network close to Oxford, they are soon heading for the ports in journeys that save a useful two million lorry miles per year. Not that rail services from the plant are a new idea as the first sidings appeared at Cowley in 1926, eventually leading to a Morris Cowley station that carried both passengers and freight.

↑ While others – 290 at a time – will depart on special trains...

↓ ... heading for ports around the UK. Here, cars are shown being driven on to a ship at Southampton docks.

MAINTENANCE

Plant Oxford operates for 22½ hours a day, and in that time a thousand perfectly assembled new MINIs will leave the assembly line. As well as thousands of workers you can thank thousands of pieces of sophisticated machinery for that amazing statistic, but just how do you ensure that machinery operates exactly as intended? That's a job that falls to the skilled maintenance teams responsible for keeping everything working, and it takes only a few minutes spent within the plant to realise just what a daunting task that is.

It is important to note, however, that the plant operates a 'Total Productive Maintenance' (TPM) approach. This means all associates, when appropriately trained on specific tasks, help to maintain their own individual working areas.

As we've discovered throughout this manual, the sheer amount of equipment, tools and robots is nothing short of breathtaking, and that's just the items that actually build the cars. Added to that are the lifts, conveyors, and cradles that keep parts and vehicles moving throughout the plant. Oh, and then there's the plant itself, that's stuffed full of electrics, hydraulics, environmental control systems, vehicle testing equipment… the list seems endless. And it all has to be kept in perfect working order if assembly lines aren't to grind to a very expensive halt.

Broadly speaking, maintenance work falls into two main categories. The first is what could be deemed 'reactive' maintenance, such as repairing equipment that has failed unexpectedly. This includes things as simple as fitting a new plug to a line-side lamp, reprogramming a robot or repairing a rolling road used for testing completed cars. The most important thing here is repairing the fault as quickly as possible, to avoid significant delays in vehicle production. Indeed, much of the work involves fault-finding and analysing problems and finding ways to prevent those faults recurring in the future. Forward planning also plays a key part in ensuring that delays are kept to a minimum when repairs are needed; for example, the shafts that operate the vehicle conveyors are belt-driven, and having a spare belt already fitted to the driveshaft means replacing a failed item takes 15 minutes rather than an hour.

Then there's the second category, which is planned maintenance, referred to within the plant as 'total productive maintenance' (TPM). Each area of the plant has its own specific maintenance tasks (outlined below), which include the servicing of tools and robots and might be required on a weekly, monthly or quarterly basis. Plenty of maintenance work is undertaken between 4:30 and 6:00 in the morning when the production lines aren't operating, but weekends also play an important part in the maintenance regime, as that's the time when larger jobs can be undertaken, for example the recommissioning of a robot cell, or solving trickier faults that may have been just managed during the week. It's all another vital part of Plant Oxford's operation, and a system of continuous improvement is employed to reach a target of 98.5% technical availability for equipment, *ie* the amount of time equipment is running.

Lastly, there's the matter of bringing the plant back to life after the two-week summer shutdown, something that can present the maintenance teams with big challenges. Substantial amounts of work could have been undertaken, from the installation of new equipment to major building alterations, but whatever has been done the first day back after the break needs to see full production resumed as quickly as possible. Meetings are held on a daily basis during the shutdown and the progress of each project is rated as Green, Amber or Red – that way, any delays can quickly be identified and a solution found. Then over the weekend prior to production resuming a small batch of vehicles – in the region of 125 cars – are put through the assembly process to test that everything is running smoothly. Only then is the green light given and the business of building 1,000 MINIs per day can resume.

Maintenance in Body in White

Cleanliness is important, as dirt and debris will affect weld quality and the work of the Paint Shop, so Saturday nights see machinery such as the panel fitting jigs and weld guns blasted with dry-ice pellets to remove accumulated dust and welding slag (this method of cleaning is ideal; using dry ice means there is no residue or moisture generated by the process, so it's safe to use on the complex and expensive equipment used within the plant).

As well as the planned maintenance scheduled by the equipment manufacturers and the planning team, regular visual and audible checks (known as 'dynamic maintenance') are also carried out on equipment such as robots, lifters and conveyors, to identify any leaks, damage or wear in bearings and belts. The plant is also working on the installation of condition-based monitoring systems that will identify potential issues with motors, gears or bearings as the machinery is operating, which will enable accurate data on equipment wear rates and more cost-effective maintenance to take place; not only will such a system prevent components being replaced unnecessarily, saving money, but it will also mean that associates can focus on other tasks. The large number of robots also receive regular attention, with small gearboxes getting oil changes after 6,000 hours and then all gearboxes after 18,000 hours.

With so much equipment to look after, maintenance within Body in White relies on around 220 people, who are shift-based, with a total coverage of six and a half days a week.

Maintenance in the Paint Shop

Not only do conveyors and motors benefit from the same attention described for Final Assembly, below, but there are also some specific operations. These include regular checks of the gauges and pipework that carry the paint – flow monitors are employed to check the latter for blockages – along with periodic cleaning of the day tanks where paint is stored before being pumped to the spray booths. The paint robots themselves will self-flush on a regular basis, while the pipework carrying underbody sealant is depressurised at the end of every shift and then repressurised and purged before work recommences.

Maintenance in Final Assembly

This is broadly similar to the work that takes place in Body in White, with machinery such as conveyors and exit lifters undergoing routine maintenance that includes lubrication and checks on bearings and belts. There are a few unique tasks, including the cleaning of the nozzles that apply bonding sealant in the glazing cell.

WAYNE BERRY

MAINTENANCE TECHNICIAN

'My original career plan didn't really involve cars,' says plant maintenance expert Wayne Berry. 'I played a lot of sport when I was younger and wanted to be a professional volleyball player – I played for the England Juniors – but it was clear that I'd need a proper career. That led me into the RAF, where I worked as an electrical technician for ten years, fixing everything from generators to arrester gear that's similar to that used on aircraft carriers. After leaving in 2000 I spent a year at Heathrow, which didn't really suit me, so when the job at Plant Oxford came up in 2001 I grabbed it. Starting as an Electrical Maintenance Associate, I was put on a robot programming course in my first week and I've been here ever since. Along with working and maintaining our robots, I am also the deputy shift leader in asembly. There's certainly a big difference in the technology from my RAF days but it's a job I love. The people are great, and it's very satisfying using your skills to solve the challenges faced every day.'

↓ Specially trained maintenance crews can respond to any problems within minutes, minimising any delays to production.

ROBOTS

As you will have gathered from reading other sections of this manual, robots play a very large part in the work taking place at Plant Oxford, nowhere more so than in Body in White, which means they merit some detailed explanation. The first thing to note is that they are supplied by two companies, Kuka and ABB, and their type and usage is as follows:

Kuka

- KR2150L110-2 robots – these measure the final geometry of the bodyshells. They are an older type of robot that was also used on the previous R-series model of the MINI, but they are still serviceable and very reliable. Measurement is done with a Perceptron laser measurement system. The cameras are mounted on the robots, giving an infinitely flexible method of measuring each shell produced. The system enables a 100% geometry check, thereby ensuring that only vehicles within tolerance proceed to the next stage of production.

- KR500L-420 robots – these are part of the latest F-series MINI installation. While they are slightly unusual in that all of the other robots are made by ABB, the Kuka items were selected for the specific task of handling the complete underbody assembly through various sections of the body shop. ABB do manufacture robots capable of handling that payload, but due to the design of the robot wrist they could not achieve all of the positions required by the Body in White processes. All of these Kuka robots are mounted on a seven-axis carriage, enabling a considerably extended operating range.

↓ An example of the Kuka robots used during underbody assembly.

ABB are the main and certainly most numerous type of robot used in making the F-series MINI:

- 6620LX-150/1.9 – this robot has one linear axis and a five-axis arm. The linear axis allows the robot to traverse an elevated runway enabling it to work in several stations. This type is used for both welding and handling operations.
- 6640-130/3.2 – this robot is from the 6640 range and is the most numerous sub-type. The '130/3.2' part of its name refers to the fact that it can carry a payload of up to 130kg and has a working radius of 3.2m. It is a standard six-axis industrial robot used for Perceptron measurement, welding and handling operations.
- 6640-180/2.55 – a standard six-axis industrial robot used for handling operations.
- 6640-205/2.75 – a standard six-axis

industrial robot used for both welding and handling operations.

- 6640-235/2.55 – the most common of the 6640 type robots in Plant Oxford. It is a standard six-axis industrial robot used for both welding and handling operations.
- 6650S-200/3.0 – this type of robot belongs to the 6650 series, its type designation 'S' denoting that it has been specifically designed for shelf-mount operation. The robots are mainly mounted on high-level gantries and work in stations below them. Like most of the previous types this is a six-axis robot used for welding and handling operations.
- 7600-325/3.1 – the 7600 series robots perform the same operations as those above but have a higher payload. The naming convention is the same as for the 6640 series, so a payload of 325kg and a working

↓ **ABB robots at work on the Auto Bolt-on Line, where the doors, bonnet, and tailgate are fitted.**

↑ Watching so many robots at work is a mesmerising sight, and is a part of the build process that never fails to impress visitors to Plant Oxford.

radius of 3.1m. This one is a six-axis robot used for handling operations.

■ 7600-340/2.8 – a standard six-axis robot used for both welding and handling operations.
■ 7600-500/2.55 – a standard six-axis industrial robot used for both welding and handling operations.

In over 80 locations across Body in White a variety of 6640 and 7600 robots are also mounted on a seventh axis which is a linear carriage that vastly increases their flexibility and working range.

Installation

Except for the LX, shelf-mounted and seventh axis types all of the robots are floor-mounted. Fixed to special bases supplied by the robots' manufacturer, these have dowel locations to ensure precise installation and facilitate accurate replacement should a robot need to be exchanged. The bases can be different heights dependent on the required working area of each machine; some are almost at

floor level while others are on plinths up to 3m in height. The installation location is dictated by the overall floor plan and machine layout, which are modelled by a very comprehensive computer-aided design process. Specifically rated fixings and bonding resin are used to mount the robot's base plate to the specified location and it's installed on to this using the manufacturer's dowel locations, ensuring an accurate and repeatable position.

The robot controller's location is also considered in the overall design. This is always outside the guarded area of the operating machine and consideration must be taken regarding the routing of power and communication cables. Once the installation of the robot and any tooling to hold the work pieces is complete the cell is accurately measured so that a robot coordinate system can be created. This is one of the many complex and important processes conducted during initial installation. The measured coordinate system, known in ABB terms as a 'work object', ensures that the robot can relate to specified process positions known as the 'car line coordinate system'.

Installation programming

Even early in the design stage robot programming is taken into consideration. As the computer-aided design phase progresses, the positions of each robot and tooling bed will be assigned a coordinate system that will denote its position within the body shop. These positions enable offline 'RobCad' programming to begin. Specialist programming software using computer-aided design models from the robot manufacturer permit comprehensive and accurate offline programs to be created and optimised. As this phase nears completion areas of the body shop can be run as computer simulations, which gives the installation teams an opportunity to prove that the process is sound and that the machine will work within the specified cycle time.

Once the hardware has been installed on site, robot programs that have been created offline are loaded. Modern offline programming has resulted in huge cost savings, as it enables problems to be resolved before designs leave the drawing board, and comprehensive programming to be completed before hardware installation takes place. Previously programming wasn't carried out until all the hardware was installed, and was then conducted over several months, extending project times and costs. It was usually only at the time of programming that any glitches in the design of hardware would become apparent, causing delays and sleepless nights for designers and project managers alike.

Post-installation programming

Even in an operational body shop there are times when modifications to robot paths or positions are required. These can be for various reasons but normally occur to accommodate product changes or as part of Plant Oxford's continuing drive for improvement in both quality and efficiency. Unless the changes are very comprehensive the programs will be modified online, using either specific robot software running on a local PC or laptop, or directly on a 'robot-teach pendant'. Position changes will require the programmer to move the robot to

the required position using the pendant's joy stick and then modify existing positions or create new ones as required.

Robot exchange

All of the robots used in Oxford are measured by the manufacturer before delivery to site. This ensures that the robot is 'absolutely accurate' and removes any manufacturing tolerances that might occur during the robot's initial assembly. For instance, two 'non-accurate' robots of the same type, when placed in exactly the same position and running the same program, would not move to exactly the same place, and the deviation could be as much as 20mm, a huge amount in car-building terms. This is due to all the machining and assembly tolerances, compounded during construction of the robot arm.

Once the robots have been measured and a calculated set of offsets applied to each robot, they would then be absolutely accurate and would operate in the same way and be interchangeable without the necessity of reprogramming.

↑ Operators can make changes to the robots' programming from outside the cells, using these remote tools.

Maintenance

The large number of robots employed means the only practical method of maintaining the servicing schedule is to use the support of the manufacturer's service team, coordinated by a dedicated MINI team in Oxford. The schedule sees servicing take place at 6,000-, 12,000- and 24,000-hour intervals, with the procedures for each service dictated by the manufacturer's specification to ensure reliability and technical availability. However, as with all machines there will be unforeseen problems, which can range from a minor oil leak to a need to replace the robot completely.

Outside of the basic servicing schedule all technical issues, repairs and preventative actions are conducted by a small team of robot specialists that ensure there is no effect on output, a team that has a wealth of experience and expertise to ensure that any failure can be rectified and the faulty robot returned to working condition.

Robot applications

It's clear that installing, programming, and maintaining the hundreds of robots within Body in White is a skilled business, but before we leave this section it's worth a quick reminder

↓ Just one of the robots' many applications. Here, a team of robots is spot welding at front- and rear-end marriage within Body in White.

of some of the main tasks that these amazing machines carry out:

- **Spot welding** – the robots have a servo-positioned welding gun mounted to them, either directly or via a tool-changing device. The robot's path then involves positioning the gun at each weld location and making the weld. However, another method is where a handling robot holds the part to be welded and either presents it to a weld gun mounted on a pedestal or travels to a specific position, where it acts as a static item of tooling while other robots add the spot welds. Once that's completed the handling robot can then move to the next part of the process.
- **Handling** – robots can have a gripper mounted to them, either directly or via a tool-changing device. This enables them to present parts for welding at a pedestal-mounted weld gun, gluing where the material is dispensed from a static nozzle, roller-hemming for a seam to be created between two parts, or delivering parts to transport conveyors or quality assurance areas.
- **Gluing** – robots can be fitted with a dedicated nozzle that dispenses adhesive material around a defined area. This process is quality-assured by both dynamic and static camera systems.
- **Measurement** – robot-mounted devices allow laser measurement of the bodyshell at various stations within Body in White to ensure the correct geometry is maintained throughout.
- **Nut runners** – robots that have 'nut runners' fitted can load, insert and tighten bolts. As part of the production process some items are mechanically fixed. This process involves the robot loading a bolt into a torque-controlled driver and, in conjunction with several quality-control processes and measurement from high-performance vision systems, screw the bolt as necessary. Dedicated quality control of the applied torque and screwing distance ensures the task has been performed correctly before allowing the next part of the process to take place.

Automated guided vehicles (AGVs)

AGVs aren't a new development. They've been used in factories for many years, including BMW plants across the world, but their job at Plant Oxford is a very specific one. In fact, the only job they have is to transport completed cockpits – or dashboards – from the area where they are assembled (as mentioned elsewhere, the cockpit is actually built on the AGV) to the assembly line, ready for installation. More than 40 are used and they are pre-programmed to follow a magnetic track laid beneath the floor of the assembly building. They are also equipped with sensors to ensure these heavy units don't bump into people or equipment along the way.

↑ Following a magnetic track in the floor, automated guided vehicles (AGVs) have just one job in the plant – transporting completed dashboards. Step in front of one accidentally and it will stop automatically until its path is clear.

4 The MINI Plant Oxford factory

Britain has a rich history when it comes to the making of cars, and to this day it plays host to a wealth of famous names that resonate with car enthusiasts across the globe. Our design and engineering skills have long been recognised when it comes to the development of the automobile, and much of that talent can be found in factories like the one located a few miles from the city of Oxford. It's a place that at one time was known simply as Cowley, but for the last two decades it's been proudly named Plant Oxford and become home to one of the most successful cars of modern times, the MINI.

Quite apart from its sheer scale, it takes only minutes within its history-packed walls to realise what a truly fascinating place it is, one that encompasses the very best of British car manufacture. Over the course of this chapter, we'll learn more about just what makes this vast site tick as well as about its history, not to mention plenty of fascinating facts along the way. I hope you'll agree that this is quite some place.

A brief history of Plant Oxford

This manual almost certainly would not have been written if it wasn't for one man, William Richard Morris. Born in 1877, his apprenticeship began with bicycles, but it wasn't long before he realised that his future lay with the automobile, and when he set up his factory at the old Military Academy in Temple Cowley it was the beginning of a car-making story that endures to this day. His company, WRM Motors Limited, built its first car – a 'Bullnose' Morris Oxford – on 28 March 1913, and by the end of that year 393 examples had rolled out of the gates of this modest factory. The intervention of the First World War saw the factory making military equipment, but following the end of hostilities car production swiftly resumed, and Morris Motors was formed in 1919.

A period of huge expansion followed, the early 1920s seeing the site grow on to land across the road from the original factory that would become Plant Oxford as we know it today. By the middle of that decade the company boasted a 41% share of the UK car market and was launching new models at a furious rate, as well as forming new parts of the business, including the Pressed Steel Company that would make body panels on site.

By 1936 the company had become the Nuffield Organisation, which encompassed famous motoring names including Wolseley, Riley and MG (Nuffield was the name of a small village near Morris' golf club, and he would become Lord Nuffield in 1938). The Second World War once again saw the plant turned over to military duties with the building of Tiger Moth aircraft, the making of equipment including ambulances and gliders, and dealing with more than 80,000 repairs to damaged Spitfire and Hurricane aircraft.

In 1948 the factory began production of the Morris Minor motor car, another Issigonis design and the first British model to achieve one million sales. And we can't forget the Mini, of course, the first example being made at Cowley at the beginning of May 1959. Indeed, these cars would spearhead an export drive that by 1962 saw the British Motor Corporation (BMC), as it had now become, sending 320,000 vehicles to more than 170 countries and employing almost 30,000 people to build 6,000 cars per week.

The following two decades would see the

Oxford plant produce a raft of classic British cars, but it was also a place of innovation; the introduction of the Rover 800 in 1986 saw new techniques including the use of separate sub-assemblies (such as the dashboard) and the removal of the doors for assembly after painting which were then reunited with the car later in the production process. It's a system still used for the MINI today.

BMW's purchase of the plant in 1994 saw the beginning of new investment, with the construction of a Vehicle Preparation Centre two years later (which became the MINI Quality and Engineering Centre in 2000) and a new £80 million Paint Shop for the forthcoming Rover 75. The MINI was launched in 2001, and after a further £100 million investment Plant Oxford would see its one millionth car roll out of the

↑ **Early production at what was then known as Cowley featured rather less in the way of automation. Car making has continued at what is now Plant Oxford for more than a century.**

← **Two very different ends of the car-building spectrum. The car on the left – a 1913 Cowley-built Bullnose Morris Oxford (the first car manufactured by William Morris) features rather less technology than the MINI on the right, built over 100 years later.**

Since 28 March 1913, when the first car – a Morris Oxford 'Bullnose' – was constructed at Cowley, this factory has been responsible for building models that hold plenty of appeal to lovers of British classics. There isn't room to list each and every one, but here's a quick trip down memory lane:

- Morris Oxford 'Bullnose' (1913)
- Morris Cowley (1915)
- Morris Oxford (1948)
- Morris 'Moggie' Minor (1948)
- Mini (1959)
- Morris 1100 (1962)
- Austin 3 Litre (1967)
- Austin Maxi (1969)
- Morris Marina (1971)
- Austin 18–22/Princess/Ambassador (from 1975)
- Triumph Acclaim (1981)
- Rover SD1 (1981)
- Austin Maestro/Montego (1983/84)
- Rover 800/Honda Legend (1986)
- MG RV8 (1992)
- Rover 600 (1993)
- Rover 75 (1999)

The plant has also operated under various owners over the past century, so here's a rundown of the key players:

- William Morris as WRM Motors (1913)
- Nuffield Organisation, including Morris, Wolseley and MG (1936)
- British Motor Corporation (1951)
- British Motor Holdings, following the merger between BMC and Jaguar (1966)
- British Leyland (1974)
- Rover Group (1986)
- British Aerospace, after purchase of Rover Group (1988)
- BMW (1994)

↓ A graphic showing just some of the cars that have rolled off the production line over the years.

2013 MINI JOHN COOPER WORKS HATCH

1926 Morris Oxford 14/28 two-seater Tourer

1935 Morris Eight, Series I

1960 Morris Mini Minor

1962 MG 1100

1969 Austin Healey Sprite Mk IV

1970 Morris Minor Million

1978 Morris Marina LE

1988 Sterling 827 S saloon

2001 MINI Cooper 'Austin Powers'

factory gates in 2007. Prime Minister at the time David Cameron would drive the two millionth example off the line in 2011.

Having celebrated 100 years of car making at the site in 2013, we arrive at the present day and the exciting business of building modern MINIs. In fact during the writing of this manual we also arrived at another major milestone in the plant's history, which came 15 years after MINI production began at Oxford, when on 1 December 2016 the three millionth model to be built there – a John Cooper Works Clubman – rolled off the line in Final Assembly.

→ **Britain's then Prime Minister, David Cameron, helps to celebrate the birth of the two millionth MINI in 2011.**

↓ **Five years later, Managing Director, Frank Bachmann (foreground), with Board Member for Production, Oliver Zipse on his right, and some of the associates pose with another very special MINI.**

Facts and figures

- In total, the plant covers an area of 668,500m². That's a quarter of a square mile, or the equivalent of almost 94 football pitches.
- There's a total workforce of around 4,500 people, including 113 apprentices.
- There are three shifts working Monday to Friday. Production only stops between 4:30am and 6:00am, for maintenance.
- More than £1 billion has been invested in the plant since 2001.
- More than 30 security staff are on site, and there's even a fire service.
- There are five health staff, including doctors, plus four physiotherapists.
- The seven cafeterias serve 1,000 meals every day.

ENVIRONMENT AND EFFICIENCY

Like almost every other manufacturing industry, car production has had to become a far cleaner and more efficient business. It's an industry that certainly can't avoid its responsibilities when it comes to its impact on the environment, and Plant Oxford is no exception, which is why plenty of time and money is invested in saving energy and minimising harmful emissions during the production process, an aspect of car building that will come under increasing scrutiny in the years ahead. Making cars will always be an energy-intensive business but here are just some of the things that MINI are already doing:

JEREMY STOYLE

CHIEF FINANCIAL OFFICER –
PLANTS OXFORD, HAMS HALL AND SWINDON

The overall responsibility for how the money is spent is just one part of Jeremy's wide-ranging role, which also encompasses continuous improvement and long-term strategic planning. And it all began with a fascination for mathematics: 'My father worked in design engineering at the plant from the 1950s, so it's perhaps no surprise that I followed in his footsteps. However, I was planning to do my A-levels when my father suggested I consider an apprenticeship, as that way I'd be learning practical skills as well as being able to pursue academic subjects. A four-year technician apprenticeship began in September 1987, ending with work in the computer simulation department, which looked at crash testing and the integrity of car bodies. The plant sponsored my maths degree, which I completed in 1994, and afterwards I began stints in various areas of the then Rover Group business, including the commercial department at Swindon, and Land Rover, where I spent three years overseeing the installation of a new press shop.'

Having also found time to complete a Master's degree in business administration, Jeremy is quick to praise the support he received from the company when it came to learning – something he sees as playing a vital role at MINI today. But new jobs soon beckoned: 'After the split from Rover in 2001, I came back to BMW to run the engineering department at Swindon, and then spent time overseeing various aspects of logistics and the supply chain before landing my current role in 2014. And I'm proud to also act as Chairman of the Board of Trustees that manages the pension scheme for BMW's UK operations, and looks after around 70,000 members. It's perhaps also worth mentioning that although production of the new MINI began in 2001 at Plant Oxford I was lucky enough to be involved with the plans for it as early as 1995, so I feel a really close association with the product we make today. Born locally, I'm absolutely fascinated with the heritage of the plant, and while the work might be challenging it's very rewarding to be a part of that history.'

- Plant Oxford has one of the largest roof-mounted solar farms in the UK (see below).
- Rainwater is harvested and used for flushing toilets around the plant.
- Thermal recovery technology systems are used to ensure that heat generated onsite can be fed back in to the plant.
- A system of 4,000 programmable lights in the body shop helps to cut CO_2 emissions and improve efficiency.
- Reusable packaging is used extensively. It is sent back to suppliers when empty so it can be used for the next delivery of parts.
- Between 2006 and 2015, investment in clean production methods and energy efficiency measures at Plants Oxford and Swindon has resulted in the following reductions:

Environmental area	% reduction
Energy usage	26
Water consumption	36
Waste sent to landfill	91
Emission of volatile organic compounds	27

Plant Oxford and the community

From the day in March 1913 when the first car rolled out of Cowley, the plant has found itself at the centre of the local community. It's perhaps to be expected given that it's employed tens of thousands of people in the intervening century, and William Morris himself would become known for his philanthropic work, including the provision of a church – St Luke's – in 1937 for factory workers and local

THE SOLAR FARM

Back in the summer of 2014 MINI announced a new addition to its efficiency armoury by unveiling a 'solar farm'. Located on the roof of the Body in White building, it comprises 11,659 photovoltaic solar panels that cover an area of 20,000m^2; that's equivalent to five football pitches' worth of power generation. In fact, the array is capable of generating a substantial three megawatts of electricity, which is enough to power around 700 homes. And not only does it provide energy for the plant, it also promises CO_2 emissions savings, which in 2015 alone amounted to approximately 1,200 tonnes. Solar energy generation isn't new, of course, but the installation of the solar farm is yet another example of Plant Oxford ensuring that its car production is as efficient as possible.

PLANT OXFORD. HEART OF MINI.

← This impressive, and very large, solar farm has been a feature of Plant Oxford since 2014.

↑↗ Fund raising for local projects and charities is an important part of Plant Oxford's links within the community.

people. It's no surprise, then, that MINI have continued that work, and today Plant Oxford is as involved with the community as ever.

One of the key themes is education, the company engaging closely with local schools and colleges and providing young people with work experience opportunities. But it's not all about nurturing the next generation of talented engineers, as there is also plenty of fun stuff to get involved in. MINI are key sponsors of the annual Cowley Road Carnival, which celebrates local culture and diversity, and draws upwards of 40,000 visitors. There's also fundraising for its in-house charity, which for for 2015–2016 was disabled children's charity Whizz Kidz, and more recently Macmillan Cancer Support,

as well as involvement in many other local arts and community-focused events. In addition Plant Oxford frequently hosts local and national classic car clubs, while its family days – where the relatives of associates get the chance to take special tours – always prove hugely popular. And with more than a century of car making under its belt there's no reason why future generations won't be just as closely involved. Lord Nuffield would surely have approved.

HEALTH AND SAFETY

Take a moment to consider the sheer size of Plant Oxford, the number of people working there in a wide variety of different jobs

➜ The plant has its own dedicated security team, working to keep employees and visitors safe.

and the fact that 1,000 cars a day are being produced using a vast range of chemicals and complex, heavy machinery, and it's easy to see why health and safety plays such a vital role in ensuring that the business of building MINIs takes place without injury or accident – which is why the plant (as well as Swindon and Hams Hall) has a team of people dedicated to looking after the wellbeing of its employees.

It's a responsibility that can be divided into two main parts. First is the formal training and induction that takes place to ensure that all associates can carry out their jobs safely and effectively. This aspect is all about preventing injuries and accidents occurring in the first place, and therefore focuses on issues such as manual handling (the lifting and handling of components and machinery), the safe and ergonomic usage of tools and machinery and the procedures necessary to ensure that workers aren't harmed by chemicals, dust or vibration.

The other part involves the everyday health and wellbeing of the workers themselves. Plant Oxford has a dedicated team of occupational health specialists and physiotherapists who not only offer advice and guidance on a daily basis but also assist people returning to work after illness or injury (including incidents that may have taken place outside of work, such as sports injuries). Nutrition is just as important, so the on-site catering facilities offer healthier eating options.

Should the worst happen and an accident occur, a dedicated team that includes the plant's own fire service is on hand to reach incidents in a timely manner.

Lastly, it's also worth remembering that the motor industry is a fast-changing one; that means health and safety processes are under constant review to ensure they'll meet the challenges of future technology, within the cars themselves (for example, the wider introduction of electric vehicles) and the factories that build them.

↑ Should the worst happen, on-site medical and fire crews are ready to respond instantly.

↓ The health and wellbeing of the workforce is taken very seriously at Plant Oxford, with specialists on hand to provide help and advice.

THE VISITOR CENTRE AND MUSEUM

It's perhaps no surprise that Plant Oxford attracts more than its fair share of visitors, who come both to experience the rich history of the Cowley factory and to witness the car production process in one of the most advanced car plants in the world. It's a truly fascinating place, and luckily for car enthusiasts everywhere it's one that can be experienced on one of the official tours. They've been running since 2003, just two years after MINI production began, and over the course of a couple of hours visitors are treated to an insight into Plant Oxford's history as well as an opportunity to experience the workings of Body in White and Final Assembly for themselves (only the Paint Shop is out of bounds, due to the chemical processes that take place and the need to maintain complete cleanliness in most areas).

At the time of writing this manual there are 11 tour guides, almost half of whom are people who have spent many years working at the plant and are therefore steeped in its history. They guide up to 15 people on each tour. In fact the plant can manage up to ten tours a day, and they'll typically see around 15,000 visitors per year, a number that has been growing steadily as people come from all over the world to immerse themselves in the MINI experience. As well as individuals the tours also cater for industry groups interested in the latest technology and processes; school and university students; and classic car clubs. There have even been people who have made marriage proposals at the plant! Whoever said romance is dead…

But there is more to the visitor experience than tours, as there is also the lure of the plant's modest but fascinating museum. Open since BMW arrived in Oxford, it draws on the extensive collection of historic vehicles that are housed in the BMW collection in Munich, and museum visitors can expect to see around 20 vehicles on display at any one time. Modern MINIs feature heavily, of course, and they draw plenty of interest, especially the electric model used during the 2012 London Olympics and an example that's covered in cow fur!

⬇ The Plant Oxford museum showcases the history of the plant, and the cars that have been built there over the years, including this open-top Bullnose Morris – a 1914 Oxford Tourer.

TERRY STRINGER

TOUR GUIDE

For more than a dozen years Terry has been one of Plant Oxford's official tour guides, and he's a man steeped in the history of Cowley: 'Back in the 1960s I joined Pressed Steel Fisher, who produced bodies for the plant. My job was to teach welding, but after a supervisory role I became a manager in production, and have overseen a whole range of cars in my time, right from models like the Austin Maxi, Morris Marina and Austin Maestro through to the more recent Rovers. I was still working there during the BMW takeover in 1994 and continued at Plant Oxford with the MINI, finally retiring in around 2003 as a production manager in Body in White.'

So how did the tours come about? 'Well, BMW got in touch after I retired saying they were thinking of starting tours and was I interested, and I've been doing them ever since. I do two or three days a week now and it's wonderful to show people the work of the plant. They are often surprised at the level of automation in Body in White – it's certainly very different to when I first started.'

← Exhibits at the museum include this 1967 Morris Mini, with a classic Mini rally car in the background (left) and a pre-production MINI from 2001.

You're also likely to spot more historic cars in the form of the Morris Minor and Bullnose Morris Oxford, plus there's an opportunity to enjoy some fascinating vehicles from the world of television and film. Remember the 2003 remake of classic heist movie *The Italian Job*, featuring Hollywood stars Mark Wahlberg and Charlize Theron? Well, cars that appeared in the film are often on display, including one with dual controls designed especially for stunt scenes. There's also the Union Jack-emblazoned car from the *Austin Powers*

movie, not to mention an older model with a special 'gold bullion' paint job and bearing the signatures of Michael and Natasha Caine. Nor is the museum space only used for displaying its car collection, as it also plays host to conferences for local businesses, corporate BMW events and local education courses.

All in all, the Visitor Centre is a great way to experience the world of MINI for yourself, and having personally spent time there during the production of this manual we're sure you'll find it as enjoyable as we did.

← One of the more unusual museum exhibits – a cow-fur covered MINI Cooper!

APPRENTICE SCHOOL AND TRAINING CENTRE

Given the complexity of the work that goes on at Plant Oxford, it's to be expected that MINI would have invested heavily in their training facilities. In fact, around £1 million has been spent on them since Plant Director Frank Bachmann unveiled the 'MINIcademy' back in 2012, and those facilities are focused both on attracting new talent to the business and ensuring that associates already working there are able to both maintain and build on their skills.

Training Centre

With so many parts added to a MINI during Final Assembly, ensuring that each one is fitted correctly and that cars don't sustain any damage during the process is a big challenge when it comes to maintaining a reputation for quality. That job falls to the Training Centre, set up in 2006 and charged with making sure that both new recruits and those changing roles within Plant Oxford are fully prepared for their new jobs on the assembly line.

Spread over two days, the training is split into three core modules: the use of digitally controlled tooling (such as the machinery used for installing road wheel bolts); the fitment

↓ The fully-equipped Training Centre plays a vital role in the quality of the MINIs that leave Plant Oxford every day.

GARETH DAVIES

TRAINER

'My job here was originally intended to just be short-term. I didn't have a car background. I've got a passion for motorbikes and enjoy tinkering with electricals in my spare time, but I was looking for work so thought I'd give this a try. And I've been here for 11 years now. I really grew to love everything about the plant, and really enjoy learning about everything that goes on here, and I've spent time on almost every area of the assembly line. The people are great, and that's really important for me, so becoming a trainer has been ideal as I can impart knowledge and watch people progress. I want people to enjoy their work and doing this role provides real job satisfaction.'

of interior trim parts; and the correct way to handle electrical connections used in the build. A skills test at the end is either pass or fail,

with those achieving the former then heading for five days of further training on the assembly line itself, where the focus is on ensuring that associates can complete a task within the allotted timescale without causing any damage to a vehicle. Those who fail the skills test have to wait six months before they can reapply. The centre keeps a record of training and workers are encouraged to return for a 'refresher' on any aspects of the two-day course, something that's especially important as new models are introduced at the plant.

But there's another aspect that's proved very popular and that's 'Back to Track'. This is a chance for anyone within BMW – from senior management to administrative staff – to spend a week on the assembly line so they can experience and understand the process of building a car. Assigned a specific role for their time on the line, it's a fascinating taster of what life is like in Assembly and might even lead to a change of career.

Apprentice School

Few companies would argue against the importance of having a steady supply of skilled and talented workers to fill important roles, which is why MINI has its own apprenticeship scheme that has been running since BMW

ROBERTO BONASSISA

APPRENTICE TRAINING ADVISOR

Rob began as an apprentice himself back in 1987: 'At school I had plans to become a professional sportsman rather than follow an academic career, but it turned out I was quite good at engineering too. Things changed when I watched my uncle rebuild an engine and gearbox on the family driveway and I knew then that's what I wanted to do. My dad worked on the Leyland and Rover production lines so he helped me with the apprenticeship application, and I went on to do a four-year apprenticeship at the plant along with study at college. I specialised in tool making, but when that ended at the plant I moved across to cars for a few months, working on the Rover 75. I joined MINI as part of the launch team when the cars first arrived, and then came the training role. It's brilliant being able to inspire young people, and a really rewarding job.'

took over at Plant Oxford in 1994. The team responsible work closely with schools across the Oxfordshire area, attending career events to promote the different disciplines within the factory, such as engineering, plant maintenance and logistics, and to inspire the next generation of students. Plenty of time is spent on forecasting the needs of

← Apprentices receive training in every aspect of MINI production, beginning with basic engineering.

KELLY MONAGHAN

APPRENTICE

'I joined the apprenticeship scheme in August 2015 after I finished my GCSE exams. After leaving school I wasn't certain that going to university would lead to a job, and with my dad working here at Plant Oxford he encouraged me to consider applying for an apprenticeship. I did work experience here in 2013, which gave me an insight into what this business involved and I later took part in the "Girls Go Technical" programme – a MINI scheme that encourages females to consider engineering careers. After this I decided that applying to the apprenticeship scheme at MINI was definitely the right decision to make. The most significant feature of the apprenticeship is the fact that there is a mixture of both theory and practical experience, which coincide with and aid your understanding.

'I really enjoy working at MINI and see myself as having a future here. Also, I'm keen to gain the Higher National Certificate, which is made available to apprentices within the third year of their apprenticeship. The management here are both encouraging and motivating towards apprenticeships, which makes the whole experience more enjoyable for me.'

that includes an online test, a centre where aptitude and teamwork skills are assessed, and a face-to-face interview. A range of different professions is covered by the scheme, including engineering, maintenance, finance, business and IT.

Depending on the profession chosen, two types of apprenticeship are offered – one lasting three years for business and IT aspects and the other for four years, which covers the engineering-led subjects. For those taking the latter route, for example, the induction for successful candidates begins in August, when they will be despatched to various parts of the MINI business for four weeks to gain experience, a time that includes an off-site outward-bound course to improve team skills. Once back at Plant Oxford the apprentices embark on a four-year scheme that involves both hands-on practical training and day-release at college to gain a BTEC Diploma, along with a Level 3 NVQ qualification. There's also the opportunity to study further for a full university degree.

Thanks to detailed monitoring and appraisal, and a strong support system, it's encouraging to learn that a high percentage of candidates remain at Plant Oxford once their apprenticeship is complete. And for those yet to secure a place on the apprenticeship scheme, there's an entry-level

⬇ Plant Oxford is rightly proud of the number of candidates that stay on once their apprenticeships are complete.

the business over the coming years, and the scheme will generally take on around 30 new apprentices each year.

Applications are usually made between December and March, while spring and summer are used for the rigorous selection process

BUILDING 71.0

A brief history of Mini in motorsport

If any car was destined to win in motorsport, often performing giant-killing feats against much more powerful machinery, it was surely the Mini. Designer Alec Issigonis wasn't always a great believer in the power of motorsport when it came to developing road cars – many car makers believed in the adage of 'race on Sunday, sell on Monday', a phrase coined by American, Bob Tasca, who was involved in Ford's muscle car programme during the 1960s – but he didn't have to wait long before the brilliance of his design was proved in competition. It quickly became a success in the nascent British Saloon Car Championship (known as the British Touring Car Championship today), when the 1961 title was won by John Whitmore driving an Austin Se7en. Minis would be champions again in 1962 (John Love, Mini Cooper), 1969 (Alec Poole, Mini Cooper S) and both 1978 and 1979 (Richard Longman, Mini 1275GT).

But it was rallying that would really capture the public's imagination, when the diminutive Cooper – a model launched in September 1961 – took victory on the tough Monte Carlo rally in January 1964 with Paddy Hopkirk and Henry Liddon. The team of Timo Makinen and Paul Easter took victory the following year, and following a somewhat dubious disqualification in 1966

↓ Back in the 1960s and 1970s the tiny Mini proved a giant-killer in saloon car racing.

Qualification Programme, a 12-month training period that is designed to prepare those taking part for a full apprenticeship.

Girls Go Technical

While many business leaders bemoan the lack of women in engineering positions, MINI have chosen to tackle the issue head-on, hence their 'Girls Go Technical' scheme. Encouraging young women between the ages of 15 and 24, participants spend around four days experiencing both the work of Plant Oxford and their nearest BMW manufacturing site, for example Swindon or Hams Hall. It's proved a successful scheme over the last few years, attracting a number of candidates for full apprenticeships including one interviewed for this manual.

← Timo Makinen and Paul Easter on their way to victory in the 1965 Monte Carlo Rally.

↙ The Mini's compact dimensions and agile handling was perfectly suited to the challenges of rallying.

because of a technical infringement concerning the lights, the Mini Cooper won again in 1967 with Rauno Aaltonen and Henry Liddon.

Some of those famous names would crop up again when MINI announced a return to top-level rallying. In April 2011 Paddy Hopkirk and Rauno Aaltonen were on hand when the MINI John Cooper Works WRC car was unveiled at Plant Oxford. Developed and run by rally legends, Prodrive, the new competitor was based on the Countryman and was powered by a BMW Motorsport-developed 1.6-litre turbocharged, four-cylinder engine linked to an Xtrac six-speed sequential transmission and four-wheel-drive system. With Kris Meeke and Dani Sordo as drivers, the plan was to contest a limited number of events during 2011, with an all-out assault on the World Rally Championship the following year. However, despite a number of wins the official team entry was withdrawn at the end of the 2012 season, although the car continued to perform well in the hands of privateers.

More recently MINI has tasted victory on the challenging Rally Dakar event courtesy of the X-raid team. Beneath carbon-fibre bodywork that resembled the Countryman, the ALL4 model featured a tubular steel chassis and a 3.0-litre, twin-turbocharged straight-six diesel engine. Event expert Stephane Peterhansel drove the car to victory in 2012 and 2013, and there would be wins for the MINI in 2014 and 2015 with other drivers at the wheel.

And then there's the MINI Challenge one-make race series that began in 2002. Taking place at a number of UK circuits including Silverstone, Brands Hatch and Donington (as well as visits to Zandvoort in 2013 and Spa in 2016) the series is split into two main classes; the MINI Cooper is the entry level, with cars powered by 135bhp, normally aspirated 1.6-litre engines and running

← The MINI WRC challenger is unveiled at Plant Oxford in 2011. Sadly, the official team would withdraw from rallying less than two years later.

A MINI CHALLENGE RACE WEEKEND

In any form of motorsport the race weekend is an exciting time and the culmination of a team's hard work, and it's no different for the Plant Oxford crew competing in the MINI Challenge. In the weeks leading up to the event the car will be subjected to a thorough check-over, with plenty of focus on the suspension geometry and set-up. The corner weighting, ride height, camber and tracking are all measured and adjusted. The Friday of race weekend is a full day of testing and track familiarisation for the driver – around two and a half hours will be spent behind the wheel – while the team concentrates on refining the suspension geometry, damper settings and tyre pressures. They'll also set up the truck and race awning in their paddock area, ready for qualifying and the first race on Saturday. Sunday sees two further races, and although it can be a stress-free time if everything is going to plan it's inevitable that some work will be needed after earlier races. And then it's all over, and time to pack everything into the truck and head back to Plant Oxford.

JAMES LOUKES

GROUP LEADER, COMPLEX VEHICLE ANALYSIS

As well as his full-time job, James also holds the exciting post of Team Manager for the MINI race team: 'My dad restored classic cars for a living so I've always had a passion for cars, and loved tinkering with them whenever I could during holidays and weekends. Motorsport has also been a big part of my life; I started racing at 15, so knowing that Rover, as it was when I joined, had a race team was a major part of my decision in signing up for a four-year apprenticeship. That was in tool making, but a keen interest in analysis and problem-solving saw me heading into that part of the business, while still making sure I was involved in the racing side.

'I've been a driver and mechanic in the MINI team and for the last six years I've been the Team Manager; which means I'm responsible for team organisation and management, dealing with the sponsorship and finances, race event organisation, supporting MINI corporate events and, of course, being the liaison with the senior directors at MINI. Doing two jobs is certainly a challenge at times, and it means putting in some long hours, but it's great to be involved in racing, and the success we have on the track makes it all worthwhile.'

↙ MINI's motorsport successes include victories on the tough Rally Dakar event.

↓ Motorsport activities at Plant Oxford include preparing and running cars in the competitive MINI Challenge series.

→ A Quaife sequential gearbox is a key part of the Challenge car's unique specification.

↓ James Loukes (left) and Chris Fryer work on the special suspension set up...

↘ ...and the engine of the Challenge car. People involved in the preparation and racing of these cars have other roles within Plant Oxford, but participate in motorsport due to a love of competition.

on slick tyres – and then of course there's the full-fat JCW. Powered by a 2.0-litre turbo engine with up to 275bhp, the last is especially sophisticated, with features including a bespoke Quaife sequential gearbox, Nitron three-way adjustable dampers and a special motorsport engine ECU. In addition, there is also an 'Open' class, which invites a range of other MINI models and their drivers to take part

All of the Challenge cars are built by a separate company based in Suffolk, but the responsibility for running the Plant Oxford entry falls to a small team (all of whom have other 'day' jobs, it should be noted) located in what's known as 'Building 71.0'. Used as an emissions testing facility during the Cowley days, it has now been converted into a workshop and race team HQ.

Having run cars in the Challenge Series since the very beginning – at that time using the R50 model – the team used to build each

car from a kit of parts, but since production moved to Suffolk, the team's focus has been able to shift to preparation and testing. And it's testing that is the first step when the latest car arrives (currently the F56 model), the work taking place at a number of UK circuits including Silverstone, Brands Hatch and Castle Combe. Typically taking a couple of days at a time, the team concentrates on issues such as finalising the suspension set-up and geometry and tyre testing. The latter involves monitoring and understanding the tyres' characteristics, including temperature changes and degradation, although as the team points out they are always learning about car set-up throughout the season and can incorporate changes following each race. The Plant Oxford team are also responsible for the look of the car, so pay plenty of attention to the graphics and cosmetics to ensure it stands out on the packed grid.

Then it's time to go racing, with a small team of around six people – all of whom work at Plant Oxford in a variety of roles, from engineering to paint – attending each round and overseeing every aspect, from set-up and maintenance to logistics and looking after the drivers. Speaking of which, three drivers currently share driving duties – again, all associates from the plant – and the team play an important role in developing new drivers for future competition. Everyone involved in the activities of the race team come from within Plant Oxford so it's very much a team effort, and one that takes plenty of hard work and commitment.

THE ROAD CAR

2016 saw the launch of the MINI John Cooper Works Challenge car, a limited-edition model, developed by the team in Oxford, that was intended to transfer some of the character of the Challenge race cars to the road. Aimed at enthusiasts of the hot hatchback, just 50 examples were built in 2016, with the new model powered by the JCW 231hp 2.0-litre turbocharged engine that provided a 153mph top speed and 0–62mph in just 6.3 seconds.

Using suppliers already involved with the race cars, some tasty mechanical parts were fitted to help maximise the performance on offer, including a Quaife limited-slip differential, Nitron adjustable dampers, a sports exhaust system, beefier brakes with Mintex pads and Team Dynamics 17in alloy wheels (wider, and saving 2.5kg in unsprung weight per corner), shod with Michelin Pilot Sport Cup 2 rubber. Aerodynamic tweaks, including larger air splitters for the front air dam and a larger rear spoiler, beefed up the appearance while each car came only in White Silver paint with a black roof and special graphics. Inside, there were black cloth seats and a numbered build plaque on the dashboard.

↑ **The limited edition Challenge road car, seen here sharing some workshop space with the racers.**

↓ **The Challenge road car outside Building 71.0, the special workshop where all the racing preparation takes place.**

5 The future

We can't really look at the MINI's future without first reminding ourselves of its past, which for our purposes begins in 2001. Just like today, premium car brands were in strong demand but the problem was that most small cars on the market back then were the territory of the volume manufacturers. But in reinventing this iconic car for the 21st century the company developed a small, sporty model with premium aspirations that was very much aimed at the younger buyer.

It also introduced those buyers to the world of personalisation, something that's been copied by plenty of other car makers since; and, once established, the range grew to encompass convertibles, an estate and an SUV, with each successive generation providing greater choice, sophistication, refinement and connectivity – not to mention a more mature driving experience, albeit one that retained the MINI's reputation for fun and agility.

But the motoring landscape is changing fast and those attributes alone are no longer enough as we ahead towards a time where ever-more stringent legislation and the need to move away from reliance on fossil fuels mean electrification and autonomous capability will become the norm. So what does that mean for the cars that will be rolling out of Plant Oxford in the years ahead?

In the near future – the next five to ten years – there is going to be an ever greater focus on both connectivity and autonomy. The first of these is becoming a key aspect of just about every one of today's cars. It's not so long ago that owners were content with a radio and perhaps even a CD player, but nowadays manufacturers are equipping even the most lowly models with sophisticated 'infotainment' systems that can mimic the displays of smartphones, provide touchscreen and voice activation of key functions and even turn the car into a Wi-Fi hotspot for Internet and e-mail access on the move.

It's clear that MINI are very much at the forefront of this technology, equipping every model with what they term 'full connectivity' in the form of an embedded SIM card that allows communication between the car and the dealer network. For example, systems can monitor the condition of the car, and if a component should need replacement the customer can be contacted and arrangements made for the work to be carried out. It's all about increasing interaction with the customer and the level of service that MINI as a company can provide, and the way in which advanced levels of connectivity are integrated with the car is going to take on a whole new level of importance as autonomous operation becomes a reality. Once that happens, the time spent driving and operating a car in the traditional sense will be replaced by the opportunity to do other things during a journey, so providing a platform that allows users to interact with social media, other motorists and even other vehicles will become a crucial aspect of car design.

Looking even further ahead – to the next 20 years or more – MINI are more than aware of the challenges that will face all car makers. Firstly, there's the matter of propulsion, and while the internal combustion engine is likely to be with us for some years yet, finding a practical yet sustainable alternative is becoming ever more important. While MINI – along with a number of other manufacturers – have explored

PREVIOUS PAGES
The MINI Vision
Next 100 concept
was unveiled at the
BMW Group Future
Experience exhibition
at the Roundhouse in
London in the summer
of 2016.

the likes of hydrogen as a way of powering their cars, they consider the challenges of cost and limited infrastructure as too great to overcome, in the immediate term at least, hence nailing their colours firmly to the mast of electrification. We've already seen the launch of a Countryman with a plug-in hybrid powertrain and it's certainly not going to be the last MINI powered in such a way. At the time of writing, BMW has stated that it is its intention to bring a fully electric MINI to market sometime in 2019.

Even with that decision made there's the issue of autonomy, which is almost certain to change the way in which people use cars. Limited autonomous capability, where electronic systems can take over the function of operating the car in certain conditions, is fast becoming a feature of mainstream vehicles, while car makers such as American company Tesla have taken things a whole lot further. As yet there is probably some way to go before the driver becomes entirely redundant, but the technology, while not yet perfect, is progressing faster than many industry observers expected.

While driving enjoyment is likely to remain an important factor for a good number of people, and something that will remain core to the MINI brand, there's a strong expectation that the future lies much more in what's referred to as a 'sharing economy'. What that means is that drivers of the future may well want to use a car but won't necessarily need or want to

MINI E

The Vision Next 100 might have previewed an electric future, but MINI had been down the battery-powered route before. At the 2008 Los Angeles Auto Show the company showed off the MINI E, a model that would form part of an experimental fleet of vehicles used to test electric technology. Instead of an internal combustion engine, the 'E' featured a synchronous electric motor producing 204bhp and 162lb/ft of torque, with power provided by a 35kW/h lithium-ion battery mounted in place of the rear seats. There were no gears – just forward and reverse – and drive was sent to the front wheels, while regenerative braking helped recharge the battery on the move. With the ability to travel 100–120 miles on a single charge, it took around ten hours to recharge the battery from a standard domestic power supply. Praised by the motoring press for its smooth driving manners and punchy performance, the innovative MINI E could reach 95mph and crack the 0–62mph sprint in 8.0 seconds.

↓ The MINI E unveiled in 2008. Used as a test-bed for electric technology it was an early taste of the electric models that will appear in the future.

actually own one. MINI strongly believes that its core customer base will want to be heavily involved in shared ownership of a vehicle, but for a brand known for personalisation that presents a very particular kind of challenge. Their answer lies in the vehicle described in the accompanying section, the MINI Vision Next 100. At its unveiling it was described as 'a completely individualised, permanently available form of urban mobility' – essentially a demonstration of a car that you don't actually own, but that can be summoned as and when needed, and, more importantly, one that will still

encapsulate the philosophy of being personal to the user; or 'Digitally Mine' as MINI put it.

There's a belief, one shared by senior MINI personnel, that future generations will be driven more by experiences than by actually owning things, and therefore the task of ensuring that cars remain relevant to people's lives isn't an easy one. What the Vision Next 100 demonstrated was that a different kind of personalisation was possible, one where even a single vehicle shared between a number of different users could allow each of them to choose their own colour preferences, or have

A GLIMPSE INTO THE FUTURE

Unveiled in summer 2016 as part of BMW's centenary celebrations, the MINI Vision Next 100 gave enthusiasts a glimpse of the sort of cars that might be rolling off the Plant

Oxford assembly lines in the future. Plenty of things stood out, not least the contemporary styling that not only retained a MINI's compact dimensions – it was 270mm shorter than the

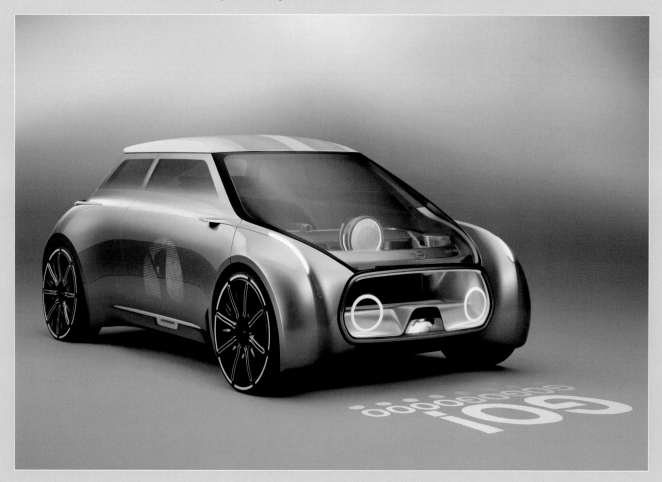

personal greetings beamed on to the road surface as they approached the car. Futuristic, certainly, but there was also a nod to practicality when it came to the possibility of shared ownership; for example, the use of strong, recycled materials for construction along with an interior that showcased long-lasting, sustainable materials such as brass, basalt and cellulose. And when it came to using cars in congested, urban environments the concept featured an interior designed to allow easy access from both sides of the vehicle, along with doors that could open as widely as possible in confined spaces.

It's clever stuff, and MINI is already running a 'ReachNow' trial in the US to test the early stages of this technology. The fourth pilot ReachNow scheme offers a new residential service, which will allow station-based car sharing with exclusive use of an on-site fleet.

There is no doubt that MINI are fully engaged on developing models for a very different motoring future. Whether we will all be sharing cars that are powered by electricity only time will tell, but it seems that we will still be able to experience the appeal and innovation that lay at the heart of the original almost five decades ago.

F56 model – but also retained the sporty, wheel-at-each-corner stance that we've come to expect. There was also a stylish reinterpretation of the classic MINI front end.

It was beneath the skin (which could change colour to suit the driver's mood) where the real surprises lay. Not only was it to be electrically powered, but the Vision Next 100 also previewed autonomous driving technology that could see the car drive itself to be parked, washed and recharged ready for the next journey. And it was just as high-tech inside, featuring a steering wheel and pedals that slid to one side in self-driving mode; a 'Cooperiser' in the dashboard that communicated with the driver via colours and could be used to select relaxed or sporting driving modes; and an 'Inspire Me' button to select the John Cooper Works setting for maximum performance when a great driving road appeared.

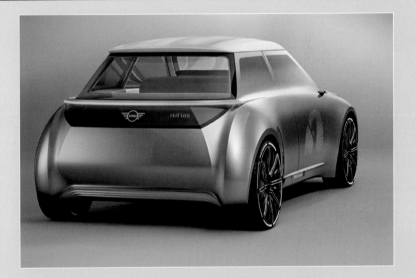

← **Vision Next 100 gave MINI fans a glimpse into the future of the marque.**

↗ **More compact than the current MINI, the sporty stance retains a clear link to the cars customers buy today.**

→ **Featuring a cabin as futuristic as the exterior, the Vision Next 100 explored the possibilities for autonomous driving.**

Appendices

1 MODEL CODE NUMBERS

Like almost all modern car manufacturers, MINI gives each of its models a code number, used to identify specific models and platforms and allow easy differentiation between the generations of each model. The codes used since the arrival of the new MINI in 2001 are:

First generation

R50 – MINI Hatchback (2001–6)
R52 – MINI Convertible (2004–8)
R53 – MINI Cooper S (2001–6)

Second generation

R55 – MINI Clubman (2007–14)
R56 – MINI Hatchback (2007–13)
R57 – MINI Convertible (2009–16)
R58 – MINI Coupe (2012–15)
R59 – MINI Roadster (2012–15)
R60 – MINI Countryman (2010–17)
R61 – MINI Paceman (2013–16)

Third generation

F54 – MINI Clubman (2015 onwards)
F55 – MINI Hatchback 5-door (2015 onwards)
F56 – MINI Hatchback 3-door (2014 onwards)
F57 – MINI Convertible (2016 onwards)
F60 – MINI Countryman (2017 onwards)

2 SPECIFICATIONS OF SELECTED CURRENT MODELS (2017)

MINI Cooper & Cooper D 3-door (F56) & 5-door (F55)

(Figures in brackets 5-door)

Petrol engines	
(Figures are for manual transmission models.)	
Number of cylinders	3
Capacity	1,499cc
Power output	136hp
Torque	220Nm
Engine management	MEVD 17.2.3
Top speed	130mph (129mph)
0–62mph	7.9sec (8.2sec)
Fuel economy	62.8mpg (60.1mpg)
Emissions	105g/km (109g/km)

Diesel engines	
(Figures are for manual transmission models.)	
Number of cylinders	3
Capacity	1,496cc
Power output	116hp
Torque	270Nm
Engine management	DDE 7.01
Top speed	127mph (126mph)
0–62mph	9.2sec (9.4sec)
Fuel economy	80.7mpg (78.5mpg)
Emissions	92g/km (95g/km)

MINI Cooper S & Cooper SD 3-door (F56) & 5-door (F55)

(Figures in brackets 5-door)

Petrol engines	
(Figures are for manual transmission models.)	
Number of cylinders	4
Capacity	1,998cc
Power output	192hp
Torque	280Nm
Engine management	MEVD 17.2.3
Top speed	146mph (144mph)
0–62mph	6.8sec (6.9sec)
Fuel economy	49.6mpg (47.9mpg)
Emissions	133g/km (136g/km)

Diesel engines	
(Figures are for manual transmission models.)	
Number of cylinders	4
Capacity	1,995cc
Power output	170hp
Torque	360Nm
Engine management	DDE 7.01
Top speed	141mph (140mph)
0–62mph	7.3sec (7.4sec)
Fuel economy	70.6mpg (68.9mpg)
Emissions	106g/km (109g/km)

MINI John Cooper Works 3-door (F56)

Petrol engine

(Only available with manual transmission)

Number of cylinders	4
Capacity	1,998cc
Power output	231hp
Torque	320Nm
Engine management	MEVD 17.2.3
Top speed	153mph
0–62mph	6.3sec
Fuel economy	44.8mpg
Emissions	147g/km

MINI Clubman Cooper (F54)

Models: Cooper, Cooper D.

Petrol engines

(Figures are for manual transmission models.)

Number of cylinders	3
Capacity	1,499cc
Power output	136hp
Torque	220Nm
Engine management	MEVD 17.2.3
Top speed	127mph
0–62mph	9.1sec
Fuel economy	55.4mpg
Emissions	118g/km

Diesel engines

(Figures are for manual transmission models.)

Number of cylinders	4
Capacity	1,995cc
Power output	150hp
Torque	330Nm
Engine management	DDE 7.01
Top speed	132mph
0–62mph	8.6sec
Fuel economy	68.9mpg
Emissions	109g/km

Dimensions and weights

	3-door	5-door	Clubman
Length	3,821mm	3,982mm	4,253mm
Width	1,727mm	1,727mm	1,800mm
Height	1,414mm	1,425mm	1,441mm
Wheelbase	2,495mm	2,567mm	2,670mm
Weight	1,160kg	1,220kg	1,300kg

MINI Clubman John Cooper Works All4 (F54)

Petrol engine

(Figures are for automatic transmission model)

Number of cylinders	4
Capacity	1,998cc
Power output	231hp
Torque	350Nm
Engine management	MEVD 17.2.3
Top speed	148mph
0–62mph	6.3sec
Fuel economy	38.2mpg
Emissions	168g/km

Transmissions

- Six-speed manual.
- Six-speed automatic.
- Eight-speed automatic (Clubman).

Suspension

- **Front:** single-joint MacPherson strut with anti-roll bar, aluminium swivel bearings and steel wishbones.
- **Rear:** multi-link with trailing arms, coil springs, telescopic dampers and anti-roll bar.
- Optional 'Dynamic Damper Control' system with comfort and sport modes

Steering

- Electrically assisted rack and pinion, with Servotronic variable assistance.

Brakes

- **Front:** ventilated discs.
- **Rear:** solid discs.
- **Handbrake:** mechanically operated on all models except Clubman, which is fitted with an electronic handbrake.

Electronic assistance systems (depending on model)

- Anti-lock brakes (ABS).
- Electronic brakeforce distribution (EBD).
- Cornering brake control (CBC).
- Dynamic stability control (DSC).
- Dynamic traction control (DTC).
- Electronic differential lock control (EDLC).
- Brake assist; hill start assist; brake dry function; fading brake support.

3 THE FIRST BMW MINI (R50)

Models: One, Cooper, Cooper S.

Engines

(Figures are for manual transmission models.)

Number of cylinders	4
Capacity	1,598cc
Power output	90hp–163hp
Torque	140Nm–210Nm
Engine management	Siemens EMS2000
Top speed	112mph–135mph
0–62mph	10.9sec–7.4sec
Fuel economy	43.5mpg–33.6mpg
Emissions	158g/km–202g/km

Other information

■ The R50 models were offered with five-speed manual or CVT automatic transmissions.
■ Prices at launch ranged from £10,300 for the MINI One to £14,500 for the Cooper S, the latter arriving in 2002.

■ The first diesel-engine model, the One D, was launched in 2003.
■ MINI offered the TLC servicing package. Costing £100, it covered servicing, parts and labour for up to five years/50,000 miles.

Buyers could choose from three option packs to add extra equipment to their MINI:

■ Salt – silver interior trim; floor mats; storage compartment pack; halogen front fog lamps; interior light package; passenger seat height adjustment; rev counter mounted on the steering column.
■ Pepper – as above but adding 15in eight-spoke alloy wheels and chrome bumper inserts.
■ Chili – all of the above plus front sports seats with cloth/leather trim; leather trim for the steering wheel and gear knob; sports suspension; 16in alloy wheels; and a roof spoiler.

↓ **The second generation John Cooper Works (JCW), introduced in 2008, was the first factory-built JCW model.**

4 THE SECOND GENERATION MINI (R56)

The second generation MINI was revealed in 2006. The hatchback was available in One, Cooper and Cooper S variants and prices ranged from £11,595 to £15,995.

■ The bodywork was claimed to be all-new, and was more aerodynamic than before. For the Cooper model, drag was reduced from Cd0.35 to Cd0.33.
■ R56 models were also larger than previously, the Cooper being 60mm longer. Amongst the design changes, the headlights were now mounted on the body rather than being attached to the bonnet as on the first generation MINI.
■ The new models were powered by a new range of four-cylinder engines. The Cooper was equipped with BMW's 'Valvetronic' induction system, while the Cooper S used a direct-injection unit with a twin-scroll turbocharger replacing the supercharger.

5 MINI SPECIAL EDITIONS

The original Mini was no stranger to the world of special editions, with numerous versions appearing during production to celebrate significant anniversaries or just to boost sales. And BMW have been equally keen to offer MINI buyers something a little different, with plenty of specials to choose from over the years including a variety of London-themed ones such as the 'Baker Street', 'Bond Street' and 'Hyde Park'.

But one in particular stands head and shoulders above the rest, not least thanks to an eye-watering £41,000 price tag at launch. If it was luxury you wanted, then the MINI 'Inspired by Goodwood' would almost certainly have fitted the bill. Produced in association with Rolls-Royce, it was powered by the turbocharged, 181bhp engine from the Cooper S and was as opulent as you might expect. Outside, buyers were treated to lustrous Diamond Black paint and unique alloy wheels, but it was the cabin where things got really special. Not only was the new model – limited to just 1,000 cars – stuffed with kit including

xenon headlights and a powerful sound system, but it was also trimmed with the finest leather and walnut veneer, along with thick lambs' wool floor mats, plus headlining, sun visors and parcel shelf covered in cashmere. For the ultimate MINI, this one was hard to beat.

↑ A real treat for enthusiasts, the special edition 'Inspired by Goodwood' model looked very special on the outside…

← …while the interior was luxurious thanks to being trimmed in the finest of woods and leathers.

6 THE ALL4 SYSTEM

Available on a number of MINI models, ALL4 is an electronically controlled all-wheel-drive system that distributes drive torque between the front and rear axles depending on specific road conditions. And thanks to a compact and lightweight design it means there is only a slight increase in fuel consumption and exhaust emissions compared to the respective front-wheel-drive models. The drive power delivered by the engine via the manual or Steptronic transmission in the form of engine speed and torque is fed to the front axle differential. An integrated single-stage power take-off bevel gear diverts the power and relays it to a propeller shaft leading to the rear axle. Power transmission to the rear axle differential is continuously managed via a hang-on clutch. If necessary, the hang-on clutch can relay torque to the rear wheels within a fraction of a second by means of an electrohydraulic pump. Fast and precise reactive changes to road conditions are possible because the all-wheel-drive

↓ Diagram showing the layout and operation of the ALL4 four-wheel-drive system fitted to some MINI models. It first became available on the first generation Countryman model, the R60.

system is connected to the Driving Dynamics System (DSC) which continuously calculates the ideal power distribution between the front and rear wheels. Not only are the wheel rotation speeds and the current longitudinal and lateral acceleration figures taken into account, but so is the road speed, accelerator position, engine torque and steering angle as well as the Driving Dynamics System (DSC) settings and the optional MINI Driving Modes. Based on this data, the ALL4 system calculates the risk of wheel slip and can then anticipate and counteract any loss of traction, oversteer or understeer of the vehicle. Taking the form of an electronic locking function for the front axle differential, the standard Electronic Differential Lock Control (EDLC) improves traction when accelerating out of bends by means of selective braking. In DSC Off mode, this prevents spinning of the front wheel on the inside of the bend and transmits drive power to the outer front wheel instead.

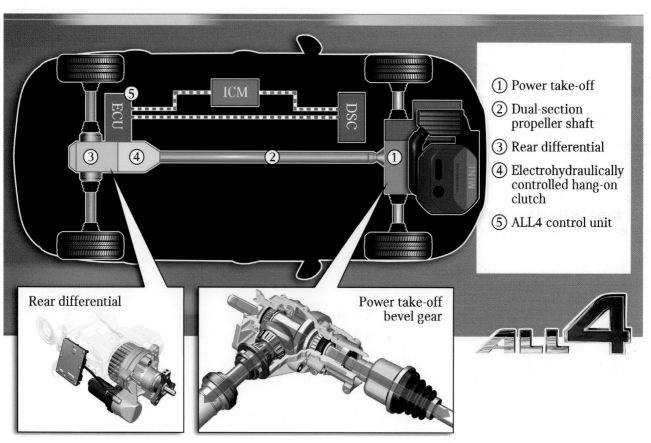

① Power take-off
② Dual-section propeller shaft
③ Rear differential
④ Electrohydraulically controlled hang-on clutch
⑤ ALL4 control unit

Rear differential

Power take-off bevel gear

7 THE PLUG-IN HYBRID

MINI had previously experimented with an electric model, the MINI E, produced in small numbers back in 2008 and intended to act as a test-bed for the technology. However, in autumn 2016 the company announced the introduction of its first full-production model to feature a plug-in hybrid powertrain. Part of the then new Countryman range, the Cooper SE ALL4 was powered by a three-cylinder, 1.5-litre petrol engine producing 136hp and an 88hp synchronous electric motor. Producing a combined 385Nm of torque, the motor was located beneath the floor of the luggage compartment while the fuel tank and 7.6kWh lithium-ion battery sat beneath the rear seats. Comprising five modules, each with 16 cells, the battery could be recharged in three and a quarter hours from a domestic power supply or in an hour less using a dedicated, more powerful wall-box. Driving through a six-speed Steptronic automatic transmission and with a choice of Auto, Max and Save Battery modes, the plug-in drivetrain promised an electric-only range of 25 miles at speeds of up to 78mph along with combined economy of 134.5mpg and 49g/km CO_2 emissions.

↑ The company's first full-production, plug-in hybrid is a feature of the Countryman range. It can cover up to 25 miles in electric-only mode.

8 USEFUL CONTACTS

The official MINI website
www.mini.co.uk

Plant Oxford on Instagram
www.instagram.com/miniplantoxford

Plant Oxford
www.visit-mini.com

British Mini Club
www.britishminiclub.co.uk

British Motor Heritage Ltd
www.bmh-ltd.com

The British Motor Museum
www.britishmotormuseum.co.uk

Index

Personnel